HOW TO DEVELOP

THE RIGHT CAREER

BASED ON A SUSTAINABLE
FRAMEWORK

By Ali Kursun

First published by sparkChief & Co. in 2020

© Copyright 2020 sparkChief & Co.

All rights reserved. No part of this publication may be reproduced, stored in retrieval system or transmitted, in any form or by any means, electronic, photocopying, recording, or otherwise, without the written prior permission of the author.

Note to Librarians: A cataloguing record for this book is available from Swiss National Library (NL) in Switzerland at http://www.helveticat.ch

ISBN 9781705421635

sparkChief Publishing

This book was published on-demand in cooperation with sparkChief & Co. Publishing. On-demand publishing is a unique process and service of making a book available for retail sale to the public taking advantage of on-demand manufacturing and internet marketing. On-demand publishing includes promotions, retail sales, manufacturing, order fulfilment, accounting and collecting royalties on behalf of the author.

For international book sales:

sparkChief & Co. Publishing

25 Route de Lullier

1254 Jussy, Geneva, SWITZERLAND

phone +41 22 346 24 05; email to bookorders@sparkchief.com

Order online at:

www.sparkchief.com/services_book.html

Also available on amazon.com and other online book sellers.

To the future of creative and courageous leaders who never stop learning and remain relevant

TABLE OF CONTENTS

INTRODUCTION Page 3

SECTION 1: EMPLOYER'S ROLE IN DEVELOPING THE RIGHT CAREERS

Chapter 1: Page 9
Are You Betting on the Right People? 3 Tips for Leaders to Improve Their Chances

Chapter 2: Page 13
Why Is It So Important for HR Managers to Score Too?

Chapter 3: Page 18
What If Every Employee Had a Talent Agent?

Chapter 4: Page 24
Finding and Empowering the Untapped Employee Potential

Chapter 5: Page 30
How Leaders Can Maximise Returns by Nurturing Undiscovered Talent

Chapter 6: Page 34
Why Helping Employees to Learn More About Themselves Is a Better Solution to Increase and Sustain True Engagement

Chapter 7: Page 39
Keep Your Eyes on the Ball! But Which Ball?

Chapter 8: Page 43
The Right Career Strategy: 4 Career Development Pillars

Chapter 9: Page 51
6 Key Challenges in Designing a Robust Career Path Programme

Chapter 10: Page 58
The Single Most Important Factor for Any Career Development Programme: The Rules

SECTION 2: EMPLOYEE'S ROLE IN DEVELOPING THE RIGHT CAREERS

Chapter 11: Page 64
5 Tips to Remain Competitive at Work

Chapter 12: Page 70
3 Principles of Sustainable Career Growth

Chapter 13: Page 76
6 Pillars of Stellar Leadership

Chapter 14: Page 81
4 Tips to Build a Career That Lasts

Chapter 15: Page 85
5 Lessons from Cooking to Boost Your Career

Chapter 16: Page 91
Why Strategy Works to Address Misperceptions of Career Growth

Chapter 17: Page 98
5 Career Mistakes Every Employee Should Avoid

Chapter 18: Page 104
The New Currency for Your Future Career Success: Relevancy

FINAL THOUGHTS

Chapter 19: Page 110
5 Visions for the Future Organisation

Chapter 20: Page 115
Why Generating Value for All Stakeholders Makes Business Sense

REFERENCES Page 121

INDEX Page 122

ACKNOWLEDGEMENT

My thanks are due to many clients, colleagues, partners, and friends.

I wish to thank those who directly supported me with the thinking described here and, especially Virginia (Ginny) McMorrow, my amazing long-time friend and editor, who was once again so instrumental in the way she directed me and helped me to develop this new manuscript.

Many clients, colleagues, and partners contributed to this book over the last couple of years. Finally, my thanks to all who have invited me to speak to them and who remind me that this work really does make a difference.

Many thanks to you all!

INTRODUCTION:

3 Mindsets Determine How We Progress (or Stagnate)

There are three types of mindsets: the one who is stuck in the past, the one obsessed by the present, and the one who dreams of the future. One (or more) of these three mindsets influences every decision we make each day in our lives—whether that decision involves work, relationships, community, or other interaction.

We all navigate through these mindsets, either knowingly or unknowingly. Just being conscious of their existence and how each one influences our decision making, is critical in the way we progress as individuals—or, for some people, fail to progress and remain static.

What Is: The Now Mindset

In today's world, the most popular mindset is the Now mindset, humanity's oldest mindset. In fact, it goes beyond humans, as it represents the survival mindset that is easily observed in almost all animals. The Now mindset hunts when it is hungry, mates when it desires, and plays when it pleases. As the most addictive and pervasive mindset, its quick result-oriented nature releases enormous immediate pleasure and tremendous satisfaction.

In return, however, it restricts animals so they do not think about future needs. Why bother about the future if now seems to be the only thing to enjoy? They do not even think about the future when it arrives, but instead react to the future when it comes (essentially, treating it as Now).

This mindset is detrimental to anyone in business or any other social organisation that depends on long-term planning and development. How can a department head, for example, create a viable budget if the manager can only think about present items such as current salaries and expenditures—and not also be able to consider future goals, requirements, staffing needs, and other relevant parameters? Or, how can employees and managers have fruitful discussions about potential career paths when the employees have no concept of what future jobs they might desire?

What Was: The Past Mindset

The Past mindset is probably unique to human kind. Many animals would not even be able to keep an extended memory, as they are mostly occupied with the Now. The Past mindset can be one of the most comfortable or uncomfortable mindsets, with many people failing (consciously or not) to escape it. Being stuck in the past limits the ability of many individuals to progress. Its heavy weight on a person's mind blocks the individual from moving forward in a positive way.

Consider an employee, whether in management or not, who has made an error or received a poor job evaluation. If the individual is unwilling to relinquish that past failure and learn from previous mistakes, how can the person improve performance on the job or even dream of the possibility of a future promotion? Specific job training is a waste of money and resources for such employees who cannot comprehend that they can do better.

What Will Be: The Future Mindset

The Future mindset is the one we humans lack the most. We perceive the future as very difficult and undesirable because it remains a big unknown. In fact, many problems we face today in business, the environment, relationships of all sorts (national, as well as individual)—and, recently to some degree, in technology transformations—all result from not having a Future mindset.

Leadership needs the ability to use a Future mindset in order to grow the organisation to recognise the potential challenges that may arise, and to creatively arrive at solutions with a teamwork of future-thinking colleagues. Employees at all levels need to embrace that mindset as well to achieve mutual organisational goals. And yet, the Future mindset must also work in tandem with the Past and Now, to understand what happened, what is happening, and what can happen.

The News Is Not All Bad

Our over-indulgence in the present, inability to escape the past, and limited view of the future are increasingly dangerous, posing a significant threat to our long-term viability. Survival of our businesses as we know it, survival of our planet as we live it, survival of our nations as we develop them, and the survival of human kind as we imagine it will all depend on our ability to acknowledge the facts and make the necessary changes to avoid an undesirable future.

We humans will never be able to totally escape these three basic mindsets. It's human nature. We need to accept the fact that these three mindsets will continue to directly influence all the decisions and actions we take every day in our lives. But all three mindsets need to be in balance, with no one dominating a person's choices.

That said, there is a silver lining. We can always make things better and improve our chances of survival by being more conscious of what we are "capable" of doing as humans. One of the best ways we can move forward in our businesses, communities, and nations is by starting to ask the right questions:

- What and how can we change, in ourselves and our surroundings, to encourage full participation in our workforce and communities to increase awareness of what is necessary to survival? What actions can we take to strive for ultimate efficiency and productivity overall, with maximum engagement of all stakeholders?

- How can we help people to escape the cozy or uncomfortable Past and pull them away from over-indulgence of Now? What "social policies" can we "organically" develop to help individuals realistically think about the Future?

- What key areas should we start transforming so that future generations do not fall into the same trap in which we find ourselves?

- What measures do we need to consider so that whatever solution arises is sustainable in the long run?

It Is All About Mindsets and Nothing Else

One final thought. We need to stop defining people in isolated groups, such as generations (basically driven by age groups, it is absurd, archaic, and mostly irrelevant in today's world). Although it is understandable why such a concept was conceived in the first place when the world was more static, it is increasingly difficult to buy into such an idea in today's amazingly dynamic and super-actively connected world.

Survival is no longer about an age group, nationality, religion, race, or gender. It is all about similar mindsets that we can find in any age group, nation, religion, race, or gender. These mindsets are increasingly becoming the main source of lasting change. They represent the new leaders of the future, those who are heroic enough to dare to change for the better.

And finally, organisations that are able to find, attract, develop, and retain this new breed of leaders will be the ones that will evolve. The organisations that cannot will mostly fade away as do those who remain captivated by the Now mentality.

SECTION 1:

EMPLOYER'S ROLE IN DEVELOPING THE RIGHT CAREERS

CHAPTER 1

Are You Betting on the Right People? 3 Tips for Leaders to Improve Their Chances

The essence of any successful business is all about knowing how to bet on the right people. Successful organisations depend on leaders who make the right bets on investments, businesses, markets, products, or technologies—and especially on people.

The following three tips illustrate how leaders can improve their chances of betting on the right people to grow their business and maximise returns for all stakeholders.

Tip 1. Don't Confuse Betting with Gambling.

For starters, one should not confuse betting with gambling, as there is a significant difference: Gambling is a matter of pure luck, while betting is a matter of strategy. Leaders cannot build and grow sustainable businesses based on pure luck.

Many people, unfortunately, do not understand this subtle difference between the two activities. In gambling, a person's skill set hardly plays any role in the process. However, betting requires the person to be deeply informed about the strengths and the influences of all possible factors that have the ability to affect the outcome of the process in question, either positively or negatively.

Without leveraging the latest approaches, technology, and critical data to hire, develop, and retain "only" the right people to grow a business, leaders take tremendous risks. In fact, without this knowledge and support, they are actually gambling, which can impact the performance of their organisations in the long run.

Tip 2. Only Remarkable People Can Create Remarkable Things.

Another important tip for leaders is to remember that nothing emerges from nothing. That is, if a company uses mediocre and/or archaic hiring approaches and tools, the result will only be mediocre hires, productivity, and outcomes. The ability to recognise and understand the type of people you hire, develop, and retain to operate and grow your business is mission critical to its future long-term success.

On the one hand, there is no point in placing mediocre people in roles where you expect them to significantly transform and grow your business. At the other extreme, placing a remarkable individual into a position where you only want consistent, acceptable, and stable growth is not an optimal use of talent either. Ultimately, you should only expect outstanding results from remarkable people to significantly outperform your competition.

What makes a leader remarkable?

- The ability to drive major transformational change and innovative initiatives and lead others—not with their assumed authority, but due to their convincing vision and highly compelling ideas and insights about the business.

- No fear of failure, accompanied by willingness to take highly complex, yet calculated, risks.
- Capacity to listen and the expertise to know to whom they should listen.
- Ability to move fast, with accurate information, and a focus on the best outcome for all stakeholders.

Tip 3. Only Talented People Can Identify Talented People.

If you want talented people in your organisation, make sure that you have talented people to recognise and select them. Of the many key strategies for success that leadership should employ is the need to focus on encouraging the most talented people in the company to help find and hire the most talented people. There is no point in hoping that the organisation can get the results for which it is striving if it uses not-so-talented people to pick so-called talented people! They would not recognise the talent!

The key issue involves unlocking and leveraging the talent in every employee, with the ultimate goal of employing the right individuals who are willing to align with the employer's business goals. By investing in tools and approaches to help identify, engage, and retain the right talent, both within and outside the organisation, the potential for growth in the most efficient and productive manner becomes closer to reality. In addition, by implementing a training programme that teaches employees to recognise other talent, the organisation can potentially reduce the cost of mis-hires, poor selection, lost productivity, and re-training.

Bet, Don't Gamble

Remember, you cannot build and grow sustainable businesses by making your bets based on pure luck and hoping for the best. That approach does not represent logical thinking. Leaders need to know better. They need to know how to discover and attract the right people to truly drive the business at all levels—organisation, division, function, group, and team—to truly outperform in the modern competitive marketplace.

To tap the hidden talent pools, both internally and externally, and move your organisation forward as an aligned team to achieve optimal results, it is imperative to start leveraging the latest approaches, technology, and data points. The sooner, the better for long-term success.

CHAPTER 2

Why Is It So Important for HR Managers to Score, Too?

Many organisations consider sales employees to be their top scorers, the employees who drive the business forward. After all, sales growth, whether of products or services, is a key concern for all leaders—and it should be. Without sales growth, business would be nonexistent, and no organisation of any size would be able to survive and thrive for any length of time. Consequently, it is commonly accepted that the impact of the sales team on an organisation's success is critically important to its long-term viability.

HR professionals, on the other hand, are comparable to goal keepers in a football team. They are not generally expected to score a goal, even though, in rare cases, goal keepers may actually do so. But this perception is erroneous, as HR professionals are the ones who support the whole team and stand at the last line of defense, as well as help discover, hire, develop, and support the right people, with the requisite skills that the company needs to score (succeed).

Although scoring is very critical for any given job, be it in support, operation, or sales roles, the key problem revolves around the agreed definition of what scoring means when it comes to HR.

Clarity Is Key to Scoring

Consider sales positions. Although it is becoming more and more complicated and complex, defining what scoring means for sales is, nevertheless, easier compared to other roles. What determines bonuses, promotions, and merit increases is clear, mutually accepted, and easily agreed upon in many organisations. For example, any positive or negative change in terms of agreed scores has a direct impact on a sales person's total rewards package, potential career growth, and even an employer's ability to retain that sales person.

With regard to HR positions, particularly HR managers, the definition is not as clear. Is it about the cost of running the HR function? Ratio of HR professionals to employees? The time to hire a new employee? Cost per hire? Engagement rating? Or other parameters that contribute successfully to the organisation's business growth? Leadership teams should make an unbridled effort to improve the scoring definition for HR roles so that these key employees earn a similar perceived value when it comes to scoring in their organisation.

HR professionals need to be proactive, understand the vital part they play in the company's growth and success, and—at the same time—take control of their careers. The following tips may be helpful in clarifying the situation and how they can score.

Tip 1. Never Accept Any HR Role (Actually, Any Role) Without Knowing How You Are Expected to Score.

One of the biggest problems in HR is that not everyone is clear about how HR roles should actually score. There is no point in trying to do your best if not everyone above you, around you, and below you in the hierarchy clearly understands how you are going to score. Ultimately, you will find yourself in a situation where you spend more time trying to explain to others how well you are doing than actually trying to achieve anything! This scenario is a no-no. Don't do it.

Tip 2. Understand How Others Are Going to Help You Score.

If you naively believe that you are expected to score alone, you should accept that you are not in the right place or organisational culture to score. No one—no one individual—can win a game alone, manage a company alone, or grow a business alone. You should first determine how others (colleagues, line managers, leadership) are going to help you score. Only then can you make it crystal clear to others, as well, and get their confirmed understanding, agreement, and commitment on how they are going to help you score.

This cooperative effort means that your performance parameters need to be linked to theirs, and theirs to yours, in a way that is clear and measurable. If not, forget about scoring. You will end up perceived as someone on the periphery, and perhaps just a nice person who seems to help others. As an HR manager, this place is absolutely not where you want to be or how you want to be perceived.

Tip 3. Focus on Getting the Right People to Help You Score as a Team.

No football team has consistently won games based on a single player. Think about a recent World Cup, where amazingly talented players could not save their teams alone, with the result that their teams were eliminated early in the tournament. So, don't think that you or anyone else alone will be the hero, outperform, and save your organisation year after year. Although a powerful and inspiring myth, it is far from the reality of today's business environment. However, getting or helping other leaders to find the right people to score is probably the most strategic thing you can do in your organisation. In turn, it will help you score, too!

Tip 4. Stay Relevant.

Even though this point is key, many people don't understand what it means. Staying relevant does not mean you should only be close to top management, hoping that others will perceive you as a top scorer (not to mention that not all top management teams are top scorers, either). It means that you make sure you remain, and are perceived as, a top scorer, even though you might change your team one day. Other employers or teams will still seek you out as a scorer, regardless of your context.

Tip 5. Practice, Practice, Practice.

This point may be self-evident. However, if you don't practice what you preach, you cannot expect to score as consistently as possible. You should focus on being out there practicing what you learn every day and what you want to improve to be better than today. Show others that you can contribute and help grow your business in ways that are creative, innovative, and sustainable. Let them see that you want to taste the same successes and be recognised for the scores you have achieved.

What It All Means

The bottom line is simple. People generally only remember and value the individuals who score, but not those who help others score. HR professionals need to score consistently so that they remain in the game. They also should ensure that others around them understand, agree, and accept how they score because what they do is fundamentally important and extremely relevant to the growth potential of the organisation. For HR to remain strategic, insightful, and be one of the key drivers of business, we need to bring more transparency around how HR—and, in effect, the entire organisation—actually scores.

CHAPTER 3

What If Every Employee Had a Talent Agent?

Everyone knows that talented employees can make or break a business. But nurturing that talent is not so commonplace, though it should be standard practice.

The entertainment industry is familiar with the concept of a talent agent, the person who not only finds promising jobs for clients, but also defends, supports, and promotes their interests. Sometimes, the position responsibilities overlap with that of a client's manager, the person who oversees the client's daily business affairs. But beyond those tasks, the talent agent/manager advises and counsels the individual on professional matters, long-term plans, and personal decisions that may affect the person's career.

My son is a lawyer specialising in intellectual property, with a focus on the media and entertainment industry. His passion for the sector, even without possessing the law degree, already positions him as a young authority in whatever aspect touches the industry. For example, without hesitation, he can tell you which movie was produced, directed, financed, and distributed by whom—not to mention naming the actors who have appeared in movies for at least the last 20 to 30 years, listing the movies that will be released in the next two years, and which ones are more likely to succeed.

On his recent visit home, our family got together to enjoy our favourite pastime—watching a good movie—which he obviously selected! Over the years, we had established an informal ongoing discussion about actors, singers, directors, distributors, and screen writers, speculating as to why some became very successful while others did not. In the end, we always concluded that the number one reason for failure or lacklustre results was simple: Agents did not guide these people well, perhaps choosing the wrong song to sing or play, the wrong role or screenplay to act in, or partnering with the wrong director. Consequently, as so often happens, even if a person is very talented, passionate, skilled, and knowledgeable, without expert guidance (and, of course, luck), the chance of success is low.

The Need for Talent Agents in the Business World

If this concept of talent agents was applied to the corporate arena, the impact would prove advantageous for both the employer and employee, as well as shareholders. The reality of the modern workplace is that the majority of employees navigate their careers without well-thought-out guidance or a plan individualised for their needs and desires. Although many organisations invest in so-called career development, the effort is mostly generic, with the needs of the company taking priority. Deadlines are pending, clients are demanding, and employees are overworked, leaving little time to conduct a true focus on the employee's performance (or, lack of it). Often, managers' needs are first and foremost, with managers relying on subordinate performance to reflect well on their own careers, pushing them further up the corporate ladder.

The role of manager, whether in a profit or non-profit environment, has eroded in recent years. Its original function implied that the person was responsible for taking care of people in the manager's department. In a way, a manager's job was to act like a talent agent for subordinates, ensuring that employees performed a role best-suited for their individual success, as well as that of the organisation to optimise performance. Today's managers are often too busy to "manage" the overall function of the individual employee and simply "oversee" what the employee produces, whether a product or service. To regain a genuine manager-employee relationship, organisations must focus on increasing value for all stakeholders—shareholders, leadership, employees, and the community at large.

So, the question ultimately becomes: If every employee had a talent agent, would it significantly increase shareholder value, as well as value for all stakeholders, enough so to make a difference? I believe so. In fact, I believe that this approach could significantly and positively affect all stakeholders.

The Cost of Ignoring the Possibilities

But, the naysayers are already asking, at what price do we implement such a concept? Critics would be quick to argue that an organisation, especially a large global entity, could not possibly assign every employee a personal agent. As a compromise, they are likely to propose doing so only for the leadership team or high potentials in the organisation—in other words, the individuals who "matter."

So, my first question to those people would be, "how much do you think it is costing you now when you don't do it?" In reality, the price is colossal, eating away the organisation's profit margins, slowly but surely. Yet, that cost does not appear in the company's income statement or balance sheet, so no one seems to care (or acknowledge). Unfortunately, if the truth were uncovered, shareholders would certainly sit up and take notice because the leadership team is not optimising their investment.

Wasted resources, in terms of time and money, result from hiring and retaining inefficient, ineffective, and underperforming employees. Continual training of new hires to replace the failed employees is an expensive proposition in terms of potential lost money, lagging productivity, the risk of low-quality products and services, customer dissatisfaction, peer resentment, and overworked high-performing employees. Along with myriad other negative repercussions, the bottom line is unnecessary damage that chips away from the company results more and more as time goes on.

Paths to Success

For the talent agent approach to be successful, managers need to be creative. Positive results do not come only by throwing money/carrots at people, such as generous reward programmes or budgets for training programmes that sound encouraging but only offer a general effort to boost employees' know-how and skills. Whatever steps are undertaken to promote the concept would not require large financial investments to nudge the mind and thinking of managers.

Instead, the approach demands some form of collaborative creative thinking—perhaps expanding the scope and responsibilities of mentorship or coaching programmes, or actually including the term "act like an agent" in the position description of managers. By giving managers more responsibility and accountability—and leadership must emphasise accountability—to help others succeed, and not just themselves, the entire workforce could rise to the occasion.

Managers would benefit by asking their subordinates two questions:

- What do you want to do?

- What do you do well?

The answers, when combined, should be able to point the employee's job duties in the right direction. It's simple common sense: By matching the individual employee with the task best-suited to that person's skills and know-how, everybody wins.

In fact, that process is what successful talent agents perform. They do not send actors to an orchestra's audition, or vice versa. The approach is not about simply getting the job done or achieving the company's goals. It's about getting the optimal job done with the focus on maximum value generation for all stakeholders while doing its best to meet the needs and desires of both the organisation and the individual. In the meantime, consumers and shareholders stand to gain as well, thereby boosting the organisation's long-term viability and performance sustainability.

CHAPTER 4

Finding and Empowering the Untapped Employee Potential

Without the efforts of your employees, working in harmony with leadership, an organisation is not likely to achieve long-term success. If employees are not aligned with the company's strategy, they may be busily working while merely spinning their wheels. In fact, rather than truly contributing to the company's performance, they may be steering it down the wrong road.

Large organisations today spend tens of thousands of hours and tens of millions of dollars on activities that not only do not work, but also drive out top talent. What organisation can afford to waste such significant resources in terms of time, talent, opportunity, and money?

Leadership needs to create a clear direction for employees—encouraging their genuine engagement and providing structured guidance to willfully align with company strategy—with all parties striving toward mutually satisfying outcome. But how best to achieve this optimal state?

Defining the Hidden Treasure

Many organisations ignore, or perhaps they do not bother to explore, two huge sources of employee potential with the ability to boost the company's profitability and sustainable growth agenda.

Source 1. The "Passively Employed" Population Within Their Workforce (The Forgotten Talent).

Such individuals are employed, as defined by traditional means, but only perform just acceptable work within the organisation. Totally capable people, they possess their own convictions, passions, values, and meaning in life. But if the company does not use them to their fullest capacity, does not invest in them, and blocks their growth, then managers do not really explore these people and what they can offer. In fact, most leaders do not know how to extract the rich potential of these people in ways that could benefit all stakeholders. In effect, the "passively employed" are simply disengaged workers doing a satisfactory job.

Source 2. Employees Who Perform Good, Adequate Work, But Who Are Not Identifiable "High-Potentials" in Tune with the Company's Strategic Goals.

Acknowledged by their managers as being dependable, reliable, and effective employees, nevertheless, they do not share the vision (or, perhaps even truly acknowledge) where the company is heading and what it expects long-term in exchange for paying their salary. Managers typically breathe a sigh of relief to have such good employees in their unit. But such individuals, too, are simply disengaged workers doing a decent job.

By not encouraging these employees to do what they do best in the most effective and productive way, companies neglect the welfare of these promising individuals. An unfortunate comparison is to consider such individuals as a farm field lying unused, dusty, dry, useless, and lifeless. But if fertilised and nurtured, the field can produce ripe, healthy, and nutritious food products that will sustain others for years to come. The same concept applies to employees who merely do an adequate, maybe even excellent, job, but have nothing to show for it other than good ratings and monetary rewards.

To make a sincere effort to uncover the potential of these individuals, who hold so much possibility, managers need to ask them:

- Are you able to live by your values in our organisation and are you satisfied with your overall efforts?
- Does your job reflect your passion, desire, and need for meaningful purpose?
- Do you believe that your mission matches that of the organisation?
- Do you care?

By identifying the individuals in these two groups, and nurturing their growth, leadership stands an excellent chance of accelerating where it needs to go in terms of profitability, sustainability, community involvement, and public image.

Identifying and Refining the Hidden Treasure

In most organisations, naturally, the leadership team is busy focusing on the overall company-wide picture and how it relates to the outside world, leaving managers to handle the day-to-day affairs of the business. Managers and supervisors shuffle mounds of administrative work, oversee employee activity, and solve daily problems, without having the quiet time to consider each individual subordinate and how that person fits into the overall organisational structure. At the bottom of the hierarchy, overworked employees complete their assigned tasks, with some more motivated than others.

With everyone concentrating on the demands of the workday, how can leadership and managers find the time to mine their employee resources and find the hidden gems—the untapped and productive employees who can help them truly move forward?

First and foremost, the leadership team must commit to caring for the welfare of all stakeholders and create a culture that will strive to align the majority of their workforce (ideally, all) with the company's short- and long-term goals. In addition, leadership must hold managers accountable for genuinely getting to know their subordinates: their pluses and minuses, skills and know-how, capabilities, and utmost personal goals. But to support this extra effort, leadership must provide managers with the time and the tools to achieve this goal without overburdening them with administrative bureaucracy.

With leadership backing their efforts, managers might consider the following practical ideas to make a genuine effort to know their employees:

Idea 1. Treat Each Employee as a New Hire. In other words, review the individual's résumé and credentials on an ongoing basis. Consider whether the person is under- or over-qualified for what the person does every day, as well as whether there are unused skills and interests that can be brought to bear on the job.

Idea 2. Conduct Effective, Efficient, Practical, Well-Understood, and Accepted Performance Appraisals. Employees typically cite problems with performance appraisals due to factors such as infrequent feedback, ambiguity, manager preconceptions, and so on.

Idea 3. Hold Ongoing Mentor Discussions. Employees today want a mentor who can talk to them, on an ongoing basis, about what the employee is doing, how well the employee is doing, how the employee fits into the company strategy, and, ultimately, what the employee wants to do. Continuous and engaging one-on-one discussions can go a long way toward inviting confidences, boosting credibility, and ensuring that employees understand their contribution.

Idea 4. Conduct Focus Groups to Discuss Overall Strategy and the Direction in Which the Organisation Is Headed. Ask for employee input and ideas and take note of which employees are creative and engaged.

Idea 5. Provide Employees and Managers with Voluntary Self-Assessment Tools. Although not all people have the time or interest in finding out more about themselves, managers should encourage them to do so. The more a person achieves self-awareness, the more they are able to contribute positively to their lives, their work units, their employers, their families, and their communities.

Making the Right Choice

In today's modern competitive world, it is too risky for leadership to ignore these two significant under-used segments of the workforce. Managers should not lightly dismiss such wasted resources of time and money when small steps—costing little in the overall scheme of things—can boost an organisation's long-term success and standing in the public eye. The choice is simple: Surge forward, confident that the majority of the employee base is aligned with the corporate strategy, or shuffle along, reporting mediocre results through the efforts of a semi-engaged workforce.

CHAPTER 5

How Leaders Can Maximise Returns by Nurturing Undiscovered Talent

Everyone needs a strategy in whatever they do—or risk not progressing and waste time with unaligned efforts. In a world filled with unnecessary noise and involuntary misguidance, it has become extremely difficult to focus. Attention span is super-limited, especially for the younger generations. Wishful thinking has become a pastime, and shortcuts are in fashion. Many people are tired of even trying and don't dare to dream (remain hopeful) anymore. These disheartening circumstances underlie why it is so important that leaders become role models and advocate true guidance, not stage deception.

The Key Issue

First of all, there is no miracle pill. Nothing comes from nothing. The only "nothing" we don't yet understand—from which this universe emerged—is what existed before the Big Bang. Rather than squander precious time on Big Bang theories (unless you derive satisfaction from it), leave such efforts to people who really enjoy thinking about them. Instead, we should focus on what we have the capacity and ability to create—how to shape, develop, and live our lives. But keep in mind, if you don't want to create anything meaningful, then nothing meaningful will result in your life.

Although the overwhelming majority of people are born with the capacity to shape, develop, and live their lives, only a minority have the chance to use a strategy or a framework to do so. Most believe this world is random, which appears to be, and wait for their turn, but miss a very important point: Chance is a question of movement, not standing still. This philosophy explains why so many people don't even bother to discover their real strengths and how they can improve them further to create something worthwhile.

Understanding the Pivotal Question

Actually, the real question is not about whether one is talented, passionate, self-aware, mission driven, well-networked, or action-oriented. The real question involves one's ability to compile these pieces together coherently, allowing the big picture to emerge in a way that drives real growth—not only for that individual but also for one's family, friends, work organisation, and community at large. It is also why so many talented, passionate, committed, or knowledgeable people remain undiscovered; they lack a framework or a strategy to create their own big picture.

In other words, we all need to understand that being "only" talented, passionate, or knowledgeable does not guarantee progress (or, as some prefer, "success" or "fulfillment"). If it did, then all professors would be "super successful/fulfilled" because they are super knowledgeable, all medical doctors would be "super fit" and live longer lives because they know perfectly how the human body works, and all artists would sell their artwork because they are just simply so talented.

Providing Leadership Support

As leaders, our aim should be to encourage, empower, and pave the way for others to understand the big picture for themselves as early as possible, because it is only when people view the overall perspective that they start believing in themselves.

As a leader, you want to hire, develop, and retain only employees who believe in themselves first in order to help your organisation thrive and outperform. There is a strong economic incentive for advocating that approach. It is not just "nice to have," but a "must have" approach to maximise returns for all stakeholders.

Consider this point: If people in your organisation wander around and struggle to do a fair job because they "have to be there"—that is, they need a job to feed their family or future plans, not because "they want to be there"—then they are exerting an average effort. Further, people in the "have to be there" group also have the potential to become barriers to growth for your business, because they may potentially lack the natural instinct and willingness to be creative and add more value than they receive regardless of anything else. If so, you are not maximising their efforts or aiming for ultimate efficiency in your organisation, which begs the questions:

- Why wouldn't you want to aim for ultimate efficiency if you want to maximise returns, which is the main reason why investors invest in a business and the right employees want to work for an organisation?
- Why would you want to leave money on the table knowing that there is actually quite a lot more left?

Discovering the Undiscovered to Maximise Returns

The bottom line is this: The foundations for an outperforming business include acknowledging the need for employees to learn how to act strategically, empowering them with personal accountability for their lives and careers, and providing leadership support not because it is "nice to do" but "must do" to maximise returns. With the appropriate and genuine support—in terms of expectations, rewards, dialogue, guidance, development, and new approaches—leadership can nurture a fully aligned talented workforce to become a well-honed, truly motivated resource that will drive future growth and innovation for decades to come.

CHAPTER 6

Why Helping Employees to Learn More About Themselves Is a Better Solution to Increase and Sustain True Engagement

Self-aware employees + Clear company goals = Outperforming organisation

Many organisations waste so much money and resources on hiring, developing, retaining, and rewarding "the wrong people"—with little emphasis on overall employee experience and maximal use of talent. As it is important to recognise that employee experience can mean different things to different people, we have to be careful in using the term "employee experience/engagement." The focus should be on the issue of "employee vs. employer" alignment if our true intention is to significantly increase organisational performance.

Employee vs. employer alignment has two basic rules:

> Rule 1. Ensure that employees are actually aligned with themselves (i.e., are self-aware).

> Rule 2. With evidence of the first rule in hand, ensure that employees are willing to align with your company's goals.

If these rules are not validated within your organisation, you are wasting valuable resources on costly incentive programmes that might only bring incremental organisational improvement.

How Do You Know People Are Aligned with Themselves?

Obviously, personal alignment/self-awareness is not an easy task, prompting numerous perspectives, thoughts, and insights on the issue. Consequently, there are multiple ways that individuals can reach their destination. Although some will take longer than others, any effort is positive if it helps one to learn more about oneself. After all, a person who remains self-ignorant is not only a danger to that individual but also to society at large—a point that many people do not understand.

Of course, while we cannot expect every person to achieve self-awareness, anyone running a business should know whether the people who are working with them are self-aware. Otherwise, managers simply dwell in a land of wishful thinking, hoping that things will turn out well. In fact, they:

- Hire people and say, hopefully we made a good hire!
- Reward people and say, hopefully they will not leave!
- Train people and say, hopefully they have learned something!
- Promote people to leadership roles and say, hopefully they will lead!

You must do better than that when you run a business. You need to know if employees and colleagues know their strengths and weaknesses, have certain values, think about their future and actively plan for it, want to contribute, have a personal mission, are compassionate about others, and so on. You also should know whether those personal needs and interest are compatible with your company.

Employees and colleagues who have not thought about or are not even thinking about any of these factors are unlikely to contribute to the success of your company. Instead, they will be passive contributors who aim for the bare minimum. Regardless of whatever reward programme you deploy, you will not—and cannot—outperform in the marketplace with individuals who only make the bare minimum of effort. You will continue to waste value and resources for all stakeholders, including those passive contributors.

How Do You Align People vs. Your Company?

Conventional wisdom simply assumes that employees should follow employers' goals if they expect to earn rewards for whatever role they undertake. This wisdom also assumes that the source of the alignment should come from the employer.

In reality, it should come from both parties, as a one-dimensional effort does not work—or, at the very least, does not work well. Consider: Would you like to be with people whom you know are indifferent to your presence? Would you enjoy forcing people to behave in a certain way solely due to the influence of your money and the rewards you can offer? These scenarios will not result in positive outcomes over the long-term and will not provide a foundation for outperformance.

What Can You Do Now?

The more that employees are aware of their capabilities and wants, and the more that they align with a company's business requirements (technical and cultural), such companies should outperform the competition. The issue is not whether people like the office environment or their boss, for example—the so-called "employee engagement/experience" per say. The right question to ask is whether employees "know" their capabilities and, thereafter, whether they "like" and "know" what they "want" to do in life. The accompanying question to ask is whether those capabilities and wants match organisational goals.

Sincerely, if you really love what you do and you have all it takes to achieve something, do you really care where you work? Think of those people engaged in start-up companies who are enthusiastic about what they do in spite of frequently working in miserable conditions, including garages, rundown offices, and the like. They possess creativity, passion, dedication, and ambition among many other things. Are they disengaged? Absolutely not.

As a first step toward moving your organisation on the road to alignment, obtain a data-driven assessment of what is actually happening in your organisation. Discover what percentage of your employees actually "know" what they "want to do" in life and are aligned with what your business wants to achieve. With a clear idea of the situation, think about how you can improve your current state. Start having internal conversations around these questions if you truly want to outperform. The alternative, if you are satisfied with the status quo, is to sit passively and wait for your turn the next time a self-ignorant person tells you what to do.

CHAPTER 7

Keep Your Eyes on the Ball! But Which Ball?

Throughout my career, I have been part of diverse global leaderships teams and held various positions of responsibility. Many years ago, one of our business leaders, who was responsible for the unit, frequently advised us to "keep our eyes on the ball!" During almost every monthly financial call, and at the end of every call, he repeated these words. "Don't forget to keep your eyes on the ball!" Nobody thought to question him about what he really meant.

At the time, my assignment involved building a new global product line that would be managed in multiple locations. My participation in helping to launch this business successfully was critical for my career. I had to prove that not only could I do it, but also that I could do it with sustainable results. All I had on hand to initiate the project was a very good brand and, of course, an approved strategic decision supported by the global leadership to invest in this new business.

From my perspective, "keeping my eyes on the ball" simply meant that I had to ensure that the business generated revenues and profits within the established timelines—or, my position and reputation would be in jeopardy. Hearing our global business leader repeating his phrase, mostly on the financial calls, I assume, looking back, that we all implicitly thought he was referring to the financial metrics and results that he expected.

A Conversation and Good Advice

After a few other calls, I believed there had to be more to what he was saying. Knowing how critical the project was to my career and the company's bottom line, I had to be certain that I knew what he expected from me.

So, I asked, "What do you really mean by 'keep your eyes on the ball'? Financial results?"

To that, he replied, "Listen Ali, what do you think is the most important ingredient of a successful business?"

My immediate response was, "revenue growth and profitability."

To which he responded, "Wrong. Revenue and profitability are the underlying causes of something else."

Considering the scale of our client base at the time, whatever we introduced in the market would enable us to sell a few new products to generate some revenue.

With that in mind, I tried again: "Well, what about scale?"

He replied in the negative, adding, "The people whom you select to work with is the most important ingredient of any successful and sustainable business. You need to keep your eyes on your people all the time. The moment you stop doing that, you will start losing." He also offered this advice:

- Keep an eye on the people you hire.

- Keep an eye on the people you trust to give accountability to lead.

- Keep an eye on the people you promote.

- Keep an eye on the people you select to fill critical positions.

- Keep an eye on the people who behave wrongly to others.

- Keep an eye on the people whom you develop and prepare to grow the business for the future.

And finally, "As long as you do these things, you will not have to worry about anything else. Trust me!"

The Right Focus

Being young and naïve at the time, his advice prompted a mind-shift for me. Ever since, the only thing I focus on in a business is on people. Plain and simple.

After a few years working together, we all moved on to new roles. While he held several CEO and management board roles in very successful companies, we kept in contact as we enjoyed each other's company. And every time, I heard this phrase spoken in a business setting, I remembered him and thought about how so many people misunderstood this phrase.

Nearly 15 years later, I had the pleasure to spend another weekend with him, along with other former friends/colleagues. During one conversation, I said to him, "Remember how you told us to keep an eye on the ball? I did that throughout most of my career, and it helped me to achieve whatever I set up in my mind. But, unfortunately, I witnessed the opposite practice by many leaders. To use another analogy, they kept their eyes only on the cake, not on the people who were baking the cake. Those leaders were only interested in getting a piece of the cake. What do you think about that?"

He looked at me with great surprise and said, "I guess there will always be very hungry people on this planet who eat more than their share—and people do need to eat. But you know that very successful businesses are only built by people who engender trust with their clients as well as their own people. If you lose sight of this point, you are in trouble. Stick with building trust. And don't forget that 'people' means clients, your colleagues, and your employees. So, my friend, continue to keep your eyes on the ball—keep your eyes on the people!"

CHAPTER 8

The Right Career Development Strategy: 4 Career Development Pillars

Career development for individual employees does far more than enhance the person's skills. If effectively implemented, the end result of such a programme is a transformation in the employee's perception of work from "just a job" to "a job that I enjoy and excel in." While the onus for career development traditionally falls on the employer's shoulders, the employee must also play an active part by making the most of the opportunities provided.

A successful career development strategy first requires a foundation that focuses on various alignments—between employer and employee goals and desires, between employees and their jobs, between company strategy and employer goals, and between employee performance and practical outcomes. Upon this base, HR professionals can build four pillars that support an effective and efficient career development programme:

1. Self-Knowledge
2. Career Strategy
3. Career Opportunities
4. Career Performance

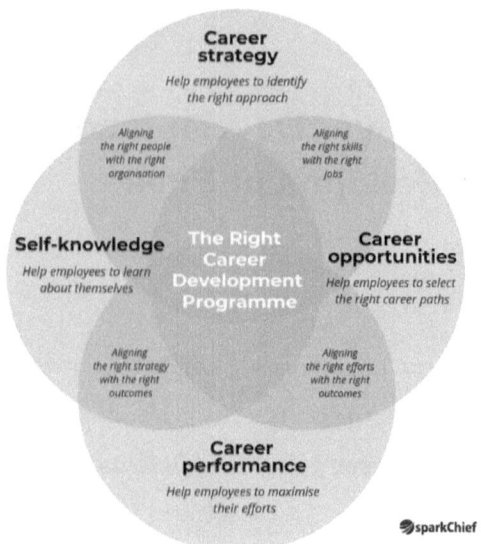

Pillar 1. Self-Knowledge—Help Employees Learn About Themselves.

Without self-knowledge, people live and work with their eyes closed and their senses deadened. Those who strive to achieve self-knowledge take a number of paths—perhaps inspired by a role model, coerced by family pressure, or the need to follow their own passion. Yet, others passively wait for someone else to discover their talents and skills and finally realise their dreams for them.

Those individuals who consider their path haphazardly, attempt various endeavours and fail to realise any satisfactory outcome. Unhappy people become and remain unproductive and inefficient—with everyone paying the price, including the employer.

Only when employees comprehend what makes them tick as individuals will they be able to successfully play their part in an engaged and motivated workforce. To assist their efforts to acknowledge such an active role, leaders need to ask employees these questions:

- What do they, as employees, desire in the workplace?

- What type of work and environment are they enthusiastic about?

- How do they envision their future?

- What skills and know-how do they need to acquire in order to achieve what they desire?

- How does their desire match the company's desires and overall mission?

- If they are at odds, what steps do both parties need to take to align their desires?

Despite some skeptics' viewpoint, self-knowledge is not simply a "feel good" factor. Self-aware employees gain the ability to discover the best job for their talents, thereby achieving satisfaction in meeting their own goals, as well as what the company requires of their efforts.

Pillar 2. Career Strategy—Help Employees Identify the Right Approach.

Possessing self-knowledge is only one piece of the puzzle. The employer needs to encourage these self-aware and motivated individuals to identify the right approach to their work life. Hand-in-hand with the employee, HR can guide them toward the career path that offers optimal use of their skills and knowledge, the potential for advancement (whether related to finance, status, or knowledge), and professional accomplishment of their jobs.

The right approach may involve a combination of steps, which employers can offer, such as:

- Appropriate training. Employees can access this education in diverse ways: through internal seminars, external conferences and associations, on-the-job practical training, job sharing, and other methods.

- The right transitions. Not every job change needs to be promotional. In many cases, a lateral move may serve best as a way to broaden the employee's skill base by placing the individual in relevant positions. For example, when grooming talented employees for management spots, lateral moves that enable them to understand (and be able to perform) the jobs for which they would be responsible offers an excellent strategy. Promotions can then follow when the individual is qualified.

- Potential relocation. Moving an employee to another office or plant may be appropriate to fill a key vacancy or skill gap. The transfer is not simply change for the sake of offering the individual something new, but change that will result in an advantage for both the employee and the company.

Whatever approach proves to be the most effective and attractive need not be the most expensive. In fact, it may benefit the company in a multitude of ways, simply by retaining valuable talent.

Pillar 3. Career Opportunities—Help Employees Select the Right Career Paths.

Having a detailed strategy is all well and good, but if there are no opportunities for advancement in position or knowledge, employees will not be inclined to stay with the company. Common sense holds that motivated individuals will not be happy with stagnation, but will seek better and more satisfying jobs elsewhere—often, with the company's competitors. Such moves would be a severe loss to the employer in terms of the cost of hiring and training a new employee, lost knowledge and experience of the company's operations and culture, disruption of productivity, and so on.

To develop viable career paths, and match employees' skills with the right positions, HR professionals should consider the following elements:

- An inventory of skills and descriptive job descriptions that accurately reflect responsibilities and requirements, without which the match between employee and position is doomed to failure or lacklustre results

- A mentoring system that allows give-and-take between an experienced person who is not the individual's immediate supervisor or manager, thereby injecting objectivity into the workplace dynamic

- Open and timely communication about job openings, without which employees lack the knowledge of possibilities within the organisation

To encourage progress—and then not provide it practical opportunities—can only lead to lower morale, motivation, and productivity.

Pillar 4. Career Performance—Help Employees Maximise Their Efforts.

All of the above points are meaningless without honest and open dialogue about the employer's expectations vs. the employee's performance on the job. Periodic discussion should include feedback from the manager, mentor, colleagues and team partners, and the employee, too. The resulting well-rounded and objective view of the individual's standing can uncover what works, what doesn't work, and what's next. Going forward, the conversation should develop future steps, in partnership with the employee, that continue to align the employee's efforts with the company's mission.

The Benefits Justify the Efforts

While many of these points are not surprising, what is astounding is that some companies discard them as unimportant. That said, when these four pillars overlap, leadership stands to reap a number of benefits:

- Self-knowledge and career strategy align the right people with the right organisation.

- Career strategy and career opportunities align the right people with the right jobs.

- Career opportunities and career performance align the right efforts with the right outcomes.

- Career performance and self-knowledge align the right outcomes with the right strategy, with the right outcomes informing the right strategy for further growth.

HR's job is to attract, motivate, and retain talent—not haphazardly but through a logical system that genuinely strives to develop the individuals in the workforce who are commitment to self-knowledge and progress. What works best for an employer may not match the needs of individual employees. The trick—indeed, the magic—is to discover whatever components of an employee development strategy that align the desires of the employee with those of the organisation. Only then can leadership hope to achieve their goals far into the future.

CHAPTER 9
6 Key Challenges in Designing a Robust Career Path Programme

Two key perspectives on employee engagement are observable when we talk to our clients. Employers, on one side, complain about the lack of engagement from the individuals they hire. On the other hand, one of the top reasons that employees leave an organisation or feel disengaged is that they don't see sufficient career opportunities.

Obviously, there is a multitude of reasons for each viewpoint. But at the end of the day, we arrive more or less at the same conclusion: There is a significant misalignment between employers and employees, and what they expect from each other. After all, how can employees be motivated or engaged if they have nothing attractive and satisfying to which they can aspire? Further, how can employers motivate their employees if they offer nothing innovative in return except a pay check, week after week? To ensure that employees successfully participate and excel at work requires, on the employer's part, a career development programme that meets their needs while providing the talent to achieve the company's goals.

The Underlying Issue

A win-win situation is possible, whereby employees can take advantage of a satisfying career path that simultaneously moves the company forward. But to reach this point, there must be an understanding of the underlying issue of misalignment. In other words:

- Why does misalignment occur—and continue—between employers and employees at all levels?

- Why is it such a common theme among disparate industries?

- What are the common causes of misalignment?

- And, more important, what can we do to narrow the gap of misalignment between employers and employees?

Over the last 14 to 16 months, we have talked to more than 100 organisations in face-to-face meetings, interviews, workshops, seminars, webinars, and, most recently, through our initiative, "Talent Management Audit Research." We conducted these conversations to better understand the main causes of this misalignment, as well as the implications for career development programmes. The following list, by no means complete or company-specific, represents the common challenges faced by employers today.

Challenge 1. Redefined Roles.

Almost every company with which we held meetings is going through a process of redefining roles in their organisation. Consider the following:

- Businesses are transforming and, therefore, so are their overall organisations, as companies seek new ways to become more efficient and cost-effective.

- Consumer behaviour is changing in almost every sector, expecting more from the organisations and providing clear feedback (both positive and negative).

- Technology is driving change in many parts of company operations, from product/service design to delivery and thereafter.

- Supplier management, as it becomes more complex, has a huge impact on the way many organisations source their production, which obviously affects both consumers and employees.

With these transitions in mind, the questions become: Do we, as employers, possess the requisite skill set or talent for these new roles? If not, how do we re-skill or upskill our current employees? This scenario, in return, prompts even more challenges for employees and their careers. For example, are current employees able to transition into these new roles? If not, how can we help them to make a successful move? One solution involves a viable performance appraisal system, as well as an effective and motivational career development programme.

Challenge 2. Misalignment: Lack of Belief in Mission and Vision.

This dysfunctional situation can exist either within leadership/management or among employees. Both mission and vision are critical and fundamentally important in whatever we do in our organisations.

If these factors are not transparent and well-communicated, the company lacks the possibility of achieving better performance from both an organisational and individual employee perspective. Needless to say, without a clear mission, one that employees believe in and support, the potential for career development programmes to succeed fades away over time.

Challenge 3. Leadership Accountability for Attrition.

Organisations want more leadership accountability from management and business leaders when it comes to people management. There is no point in designing a career development programme if leadership does not support it, does not understand how it works, does not care whether it is effective, and does not believe in it. In many cases, when a person voluntarily leaves the organisation, the evident lack of leadership accountability is visible.

But this situation is improving, as more and more companies make leadership accountable for such outcomes. Such progressive companies encourage management to pay more attention to developing talented employees and ensuring that difficult career development conversations actually take place. The result may well be improved public image, higher market share, happier shareholders, and employee satisfaction.

Challenge 4. Lack of Self-knowledge and Detachment from Responsibility.

This factor is probably the most important ingredient of any career development programme. The majority of employers with which we spoke expect their employees to be in charge of, or accountable for, their personal and career development in the same way that they expect them to take care of their own health. In other words, they expect employees to be responsible for their skill and career growth and to discover what they lack in terms of self-knowledge—not something very easy and simple to do.

From an employer's perspective, this lack of ownership of one's career is essentially a detachment of responsibility by the employee. When that occurs, it is easy to understand why many career development programmes do not provide the performance results that many companies seek. If employees are self-ignorant about their qualities and desires, wasting money and time on development programmes is futile. Self-knowledge is critical for the employer-employee relationship.

Challenge 5. Lack of Long-term Thinking.

This problem, of only solving immediate issues, should not come as a surprise to many people today. Short-term thinking is present in many organisations at all levels, from top to bottom. Unfortunately, without long-term vision and strategy, employers cannot design successful career development programmes either.

If management does not know what it wants to achieve in the future, how can the company attract and hire the requisite talent? Common sense implies that we need to move away from this thinking very rapidly. A combination of short- and long-term planning is essential for both immediate and future success.

Challenge 6. Unfocused Assessments.

And lastly, there is too much attention on assessments that are too vague. For example, many companies use strength and weakness, or personality, assessments in isolation. Although these evaluations are all good and necessary, their impact remains very limited (or even negligible) if conducted in isolation.

From an individual standpoint, knowing your personality type or your strengths is, of course, beneficial. But, in no way can any of this information alone help an individual significantly progress along the desired career path. Self-knowledge, combined with an assessment of talent the company requires, is a step in the right direction.

The Importance of Alignment

Without an effective balance of vision and need between employer and employee, the cost of misalignment can be significant in terms of wasted resources, ineffective training, misdirected rewards, lower productivity, customer dissatisfaction, and more. All of these results are possible if the company and its workforce do not walk the same path of shared goals.

The many-faceted solution to misalignment requires accountability, clear goals, mutual respect, open dialogue, knowledge, and talent. Without these and other items, neither company nor employee can move toward a sustainable future in which employers offer fulfilling opportunities and employees become and remain engaged—all designed to achieve ultimate business goals. The bottom line is that we need better and more sustainable strategies to address the career development challenges we face today.

CHAPTER 10

The Single Most Important Success Factor for Any Career Development Programme: The Rules

The main source of frustration for many people, with regard to career development today, is essentially about the rules of the game—or, lack of them.

Consider this thought: If we all know the rules, and if the rules apply to everyone and are respected by everyone, then we all have a chance to progress in our chosen field. However, if there are no rules—or, perhaps, only half-baked rules, or a situation where some rules apply to one group but not all, or the rules are respected by some and not all—then it becomes apparent that the only people who can advance in their careers are the ones whom management arbitrarily favours or who dismiss the rules.

The latter scenarios do not offer a healthy climate in which an individual can succeed, nor does it provide a solid foundation on which an employer can build and maintain a sustainable career development programme. Ultimately, the most important success factor for any such programme is assurance that not only do rules exist, but also a governance body is in place to monitor how and when the rules are applied or ignored.

The Real World: Rules Exist

An excellent example appears in the sports world, say, tennis. No matter how proficient a player may be, the same rules apply to all players and competitors. The difference between world number 1 tennis player and world number 1,000 has nothing to do with chance or fate, networking with the right people in the field, harming other players in some way to advance one's interest, arbitrary decisions from a referee, or intimidation of other players. In tennis, as in all sports, rules exist, and they are applicable to every participant, regardless of the level of expertise and talent. Essentially, their talent is the distinguishing factor.

In order for talent to flourish and express itself truly, we need an environment in which the rules are equivalent for everyone. After all, the concept of "equal opportunity" means fair competition.

Sports is just one arena that is useful as an example. Professionals, in fields such as accounting, must abide by very strict rules and procedures to avoid noncompliance with ethical and professional standards. In fact, in nearly every type of business or association or other entity, some form of rules and management policies are in place—restrictions that all who participate are obliged to honor and comply with.

Career Development Programmes: Rules Are Iffy

Unfortunately, a majority of organisations today do not even consider establishing a set of rules to govern how employees could potentially move forward in their careers. Many do not have a governing body to monitor the programme's success either. The reasons vary:

- The programme might be new and in an infancy stage.

- The professionals in HR might be newcomers, with little or no practical experience in developing and implementing such programmes.

- Management oversight is little to none for any number of reasons: no time, budget, or interest.

- Leadership may only pay "lip service" to offering such a programme to the workforce.

- Internal career development managers might be overwhelmed by daily tasks and unable to focus on enhancing the programme or determining whether it even works.

That said, it takes little effort to create simple and feasible policy rules for any career development programme. A few suggestions might include the following:

- Management should provide examples of clear career paths for key jobs to all employees so that everyone knows how typical careers develop within the organisation.

- Management should ensure that detailed employee career development plans are included in performance reviews.

- Employees and supervisors should have regular discussions every quarter about the individual's progress against career development goals.

- All employees and supervisors must attend at least one information session on the subject during a calendar year.

- There should be regular checks on succession plans to ensure that employees who are considered "potential candidates" actually possess the technical skills, behavioural competencies, and the knowledge required for those succession roles.

The Bottom Line

The particulars of the rules do not matter as long as they are fair, reasonable, and clearly understood and respected by everyone in the organisation. Establishing a practical and workable set of rules represents a key factor to boost the success of your career development programme.

No matter how much data HR uses, or how scientific and proficient HR professionals believe themselves to be, the real difference in career development programme success depends on the existence and application of programme rules. Any HR programme without a framework of rules is just a fallacy and cannot succeed.

SECTION 2:

EMPLOYEE'S ROLE IN DEVELOPING THE RIGHT CAREERS

CHAPTER 11

5 Tips to Remain Competitive at Work

Competition is fierce, no matter the level or function of your job or the industry in which you work. To stay competitive in the workplace, as well as make a favourable impression to your employer and boost your potential for promotion, consider these practical pointers.

Point 1. Focus on Building Only Trusted Networks.

In your personal or professional life, if you want sustainable and lasting relationships that support you whenever you need them, you must opt for "trusted networks." Without trust, your so-called "network" is simply worthless. To clearly understand the huge difference between these two concepts, think about hosting services as an analogy:

- Hosting service providers typically promote their service redundancy ratios as 99.9% redundant, thereby guaranteeing availability of their services 99.9% of the time. In other words, they take every precaution—such as redundant servers, secure location, and other relevant security protocols—to ensure that every time you make a request, their servers will respond 99.9% of the time. That's a "trusted network."

- If they did not care about redundancy ratios, they could just link a few cables to any server in any given location and claim that you are connected to their hosting services. However, the response to your requests would not be guaranteed. That is just a "network."

With people on social media today claiming multiple connections to expand their business networks, be mindful with whom you connect. If your networking is relevant to your career in terms of exchanging ideas and expanding business development, be sure to create a network with individuals who are either recommended or whom you know you can trust. After all, you need trustworthy people for honest feedback and dialogue. Network members can offer valuable insight if the relationship is based on true, independent, and authentic communication.

That said, be wary of solely connecting people who "like" you, who share mutual respect and affection, as they are more likely to only offer positive feedback. Individuals with very different ideas and opinions can provide a decided advantage by prompting you to reconsider your views and any negative perspectives you may have overlooked.

Point 2. Face Clients No Matter What.

From leadership's standpoint, you represent the company to outsiders (clients and customers) who invest in and purchase your products and services. In exchange for their monetary outlay, clients expect quality, reliability, and communication.

Client-centricity should be at the core of any employee's job. It is advantageous for the client, the company, and the employee in the long run. As a matter of perspective, every employee can find a linkage between what one does and how that impacts clients—for example, whether in direct contact as a sales person, or as an employee who manufactures a product that goes to the client, or in another capacity.

Regardless of one's function, it is critical for every employee to think always about clients, get exposed to clients and what they need, service them with quality, and remain in contact with them. If you don't make clients your focus point, you don't have much to contribute either to the company or to yourself. Consequently, your position will become more vulnerable in the future. Making clients your focus engenders credibility and trust, with the added bonus of boosting the client's favourable opinion of the company going forward.

Point 3. Know How to Articulate Ideas.

Ideas, and their actualisation, create the foundation for a company's long-term viability and competitiveness. As an employee, the need for you to be creative is essential to career success. Therefore, you should discover and use whatever vehicle allows you to be innovative—quiet time, dialogue or brainstorming, research, industry conferences, and so on.

But don't stop there. Having an idea is only the initial step. You must be sufficiently articulate so others can appreciate your idea and fully understand what your concept entails. And that requires you to know your idea inside and out so you can address any questions from colleagues, clients, and leadership.

Going one step further, you also need to know whom you should approach with your ideas. What individual will consider your idea with an open mind? Finding the right sponsor can make the right idea a reality, thereby benefiting both parties, as well as the company's image as a forward-thinking entity.

Point 4. Always Consider the Future of Your Actions.

Don't only think short-term because every action leads to something else. When faced with a problem to be resolved, react with logic, not emotion. Consider all potential outcomes and comprehend the implications of what you wish to accomplish. Think carefully about how your plan can potentially affect other individuals in your organisation, not just you alone.

But it is not only the actions or steps you take that have an impact. Taking no action has ramifications, too. In addition, your words, whether positive or negative, can be influential down the road. So, in terms of action, non-action, verbalisation—whatever you choose—always be mindful of the future. As the saying proclaims, "what goes around, comes around."

Point 5. Never Stop Learning.

Knowledge is power. Not only is continuing your education advantageous for your personal development and satisfaction, leadership will view you as an intelligent individual with potential and an open mind. Further, more knowledge can lead to career options you might never have considered.

Educational resources, such as conferences and seminars, provide opportunities for networking with like-minded colleagues. Exchanging ideas and bringing new skills back to the workplace can enhance the value you offer the company. Management not only depends on valuable employees who are enthusiastic about honing their skills and talents, they also look favourably on such individuals when it comes to promotions and rewards.

Be Competitive—and Stay Competitive

It's not enough to just be good at your job. You should excel, first of all for your own well-being, and secondly, to acknowledge that there are other talented people who may be just as good (or, better!) than you.

To ensure a long-term, satisfying career path, become a valuable asset, not an unwanted detriment. The right path involves trust, credibility, innovation, insight, and self-development. Show leadership what you can do—for yourself, for your clients, and for your team mates.

CHAPTER 12

3 Principles of Sustainable Career Growth

Motivated people seek career growth, not stagnation. But even motivated and engaged employees may not know how best to achieve that growth for the long-term. Just wishing and dreaming about the perfect job is not the solution. It takes effort, a solid strategy, intelligence, and focus. The following three principles offer a practical starting point toward reaching your goal of whatever you envision for a sustainable and satisfying career path—no matter your field of expertise.

Principle 1. Invest in Developing a Comprehensive Strategy Instead of Short-Cuts.

Conceiving a strategy to achieve some objective is no easy task. It requires, foremost, a deep understanding of what you are trying to do, along with patience, persistence, agility, and commitment to reach optimal results. Most people, unfortunately, fail to execute their strategy, and then blame that strategy for their failure. However, failing in execution might not always signal that you have not done a great job in conceiving that strategy in the first place.

In a world where it seems that others somehow get "lucky" first and then act as if they were strategic, it becomes even more difficult and frustrating to commit to a strategy. The result is that many people default to waiting for their "lucky strikes" or mostly focus their energy on short-cuts, thereby delaying their creation of a broader strategy. After all, many people believe that once they get their "lucky strike" or discover a so-called short-cut, they could easily act upon it without needing a comprehensive strategic approach at all! Why bother and make the effort if things seem to be going well by just tapping into their shortcut toolbox when needed?

The truth is that short-cuts are practical in general, but only if they lead to efficiency. Otherwise, they could easily be deceptive when it comes to achieving sustainable positive outcomes.

So, the fuss about the importance of being "strategic" means very different things to different people. For example, a good number of people believe that "networking" must be their main strategy to achieve any successful outcome. After all, the "networking theme" is probably the most referred-to narrative in the majority of stories that individuals tell about their career success. For example:

- The not-so-successful but hard-working person meets a visionary and super successful business person, they connect, and they build super-successful businesses happily thereafter.

- Or, the undiscovered employee meets the big boss at an event, the boss is impressed, and, suddenly, the formerly undiscovered employee is promoted and becomes one of the most important leaders at the firm.

Do these things really happen? The answer is yes, they do really happen! But what we need to keep in mind also is that people win lotteries, too! So, does that mean everyone will win a lottery one day? Of course not. Does anyone who meets the big boss get promoted? Of course not. Does every hard-working person who meets with visionary business people build successful careers? Of course not.

So, the first thing to realise is that although having a lucky-strike is extremely important in achieving any successful outcome, there is absolutely no formula for becoming lucky at all times. That would be the same thing as saying randomness is a matter of order. It simply is not.

Principle 2. Validate Your Conceived Strategy with Others.

The second most critical principle for establishing a sustainable career development is to ensure that you validate your conceived strategy with others around you. Many people fall short in taking this step. After all, it is one thing to conceive a strategy based on one's knowledge, understanding, and convictions. It is quite another to validate that strategy based on how others perceive it.

For best results, consider validation or confirmation as a matter of transparency and openness. The more transparent and open you are about your career strategy, the more competitive, supportive, and sustainable it will be in the long run.

There is no point in convincing yourself that you have the best strategy to move forward if you have not sought out validation. Seek truthful feedback and appreciate it as the best gift you'll ever receive. In general, when people look in the mirror, they only see what they want to see, not necessarily what they should be seeing. There is a big difference between the two. You should not skip this step, as it is important—as well as educational and advantageous—to hear how others around you perceive your strategy. A broader view from intelligent individuals can help you avoid needless errors that your own perspective might not perceive.

Further, don't believe people who say you should just do what you think is good for you and don't listen to others. That rhetoric belongs to ancient myths. However, you should, of course, do what you think is good and beneficial for you since it's your call. That said, at the very least, you should obtain a realistic indication of how your strategy appears from the outside before deciding where to begin. Your efforts will have a better chance of success if you first validate the strategy and then fine-tune it.

Principle 3. Stop Doing Just Anything, and Start Doing Only What Needs to Be Done.

Once you have conceived and validated your strategy you are ready to make choices. If your idea is sound and solid, the process should be fairly easy. However, if you have not done your earlier homework, you will find yourself dragged into things that you should not be doing. So many people fall into this trap because they believe that they need to do as many things (often, unnecessary and wasteful) as they can to advance their career. That effort is a great indicator that shows they did not have a good strategy to start with. In essence, any strategy is all about making specific choices. If not, you wouldn't need one.

So, if you have a good strategy, you will know exactly what you need to do—which actions to take to achieve whatever you want to achieve. The sum of all your focused actions when synched with the rest of your desires and wants in terms of your career growth will, by default, lead you to success because of its natural evolution.

People Need a Strategy, Not Isolated Advice

The bottom line is simple: It is much easier to develop a narrative about how others succeeded in their career in the past than what is most probably going to happen in the future specifically for you.

Isolated advice, unfortunately, does not lead to any verifiable success formula. When people give advice to others, they usually refer to just the symptoms of success and not necessarily to verifiable causes of success. And most importantly, by doing so, they indirectly lead others towards unintended failures or frustrations in many cases. People perceive and accept isolated advice because it fits perfectly well to the definition of "shortcuts."

We all love short-cuts and encourage everyone around us to find and leverage shortcuts to achieve outcomes. When one is surrounded by such widely accepted perspectives, it becomes even more difficult for many to grasp the difference between a solid strategy and isolated advice.

In other words, employers need to teach their employees how to develop a strategy to catch a fish. That means, employers must stop giving their employees the illusion that they can catch a fish any day without explaining how to actually catch the fish in the first place. A viable objective, a solid strategy, and practical steps will lead to a career that is sustainable in the long-term, offering success and engagement. That result can only benefit both employees and leadership.

CHAPTER 13

6 Pillars of Stellar Leadership

The definition of leadership is evolving at a rapid pace as change drives every aspect of business. Evolution in technology, consumer behaviour, employee expectations, and stakeholder management all force leaders, at any organisational level, to modify the way they lead others around them. Therefore, the need to upgrade leadership skills is increasingly becoming not only a necessity but also a requirement in every organisation to sustain successful outcomes.

With that context in mind, consider these six key areas in which today's leaders must absolutely become masters.

Pillar 1. Self-knowledge.

Leaders without a full comprehension of their own capabilities and limits are bound to fade into oblivion. If one does not even know how to learn about one's self, how can one can even preach to others to achieve positive outcomes?

It is common sense. The more self-aware and empowered individuals feel, the more they can develop significantly better individual performance, as well as organisational results. Without leadership's self-knowledge, corporations will continue to waste and miss opportunities for the foreseeable future. That self-knowledge, in turn, works downward through all levels to encourage and support the self-knowledge efforts of individual employees. Self-aware leaders, hand-in-hand with self-aware employees, form the optimal partnership to drive the organisation toward long-term sustainable success.

Pillar 2. Compassion.

Stellar leaders care about people; weak leaders drain people. A leader who does not care about others cannot coach, develop, and provide opportunities to others—and, therefore, cannot be a stellar leader.

Without compassion, actions undertaken by leadership to optimise individual output may simply fall short and fail to achieve their intended goal. Intelligent employees are adept at determining whether an employer's efforts to guide them are shallow and short-term, without honest regard for their future development. Leaders at any level without compassion operate solely as machines, without the hearts that could transform the organisation.

Finally, that compassion that stellar leaders show toward others in the organisation should also extend to themselves. How can one care about others without first caring about oneself?

Pillar 3. Clarity.

Stellar leaders are clear about where they want to go and with whom they can get there. They will not take people to places where they are not supposed to be. This effort demands a clear mission and well-defined steps to reach the organisation's objectives.

However, accompanying that precise roadmap, true leaders acknowledge the skill level of each individual, recognising that not everyone is capable of reaching the organisation's objectives. All employees, encouraged by stellar leaders and colleagues, strive to do their best within the honest limitations of their capabilities. The best leaders help individuals find the right position within the organisation—or, if there is no best spot, to ease them into a better fit elsewhere.

Pillar 4. Transparency.

Stellar leaders always aim at making objective decisions based on facts and data, not emotions (although intuition, based on valid experience, may also come into play). Therefore, transparency is the foundation of their decision-making process, as they seek the best results, excluding any bias driven by self-interest.

Thought leaders do not hide behind a title, pronouncing judgment just because of their status within the organisation. When reaching a decision, stellar leaders listen to knowledgeable experts within (and external, if appropriate) the organisation, gather all pertinent facts, consider alternatives and options, and explain the rationale behind their decisions through transparent actions. They do not proclaim "this is so," but rather "this is so, and here's why."

Pillar 5. Credibility.

Stellar leaders are only interested in building "trusted networks," not just any "network" for the sake of creating one. Therefore, building long-term relationships based on mutually beneficial outcomes is at the core of their credibility, thereby offering value for both parties.

Honest and transparent efforts to develop sustainable relationships at the top encourage the same kind of action through all levels of the workforce. For example, management may encourage the development of partnership between departments that may not have ever cooperated before but are now necessary to join hands to drive the company forward.

In addition, stellar leaders do not merely create these networks and walk away, leaving employees to go forward without support. They lead by practical example and action. Their efforts are not hollow and, instead, ring true.

Pillar 6. Curiosity.

Stellar leaders encourage creativity and embrace open-mindedness to boost innovation and inclusiveness to leverage potential across the organisation. Their supportive actions target all employees, not just the few top talents.

Individual employees reveal different interests and abilities, all of which should be harnessed to achieve a positive outcome for their own personal development, as well as to support the organisation's mission. After all, as the best idea can emerge from anyone in the organisation, stellar individuals recognise and encourage active participation in all areas of operation. True leadership acknowledges not only the value of all individuals but also their need to be able to voice their ideas and opinions without fear of ridicule.

Building on the 6 Pillars

With a solid foundation in place—incorporating self-knowledge, compassion, clarity, transparency, credibility, and curiosity—stellar individuals can lead by example. Their efforts can transform a mediocre, just-surviving organisation into a state-of-the-art industry leader that optimises the talents of every individual. True leaders (whether executives, managers, supervisors, or unit heads) do not concern themselves with simply being "boss" but rather with a clear understanding of what it means to "lead." A boss does not engender loyalty and top effort; a true leader does.

CHAPTER 14

4 Tips to Build a Career That Lasts

Many individuals genuinely want to create a long-term and satisfactory career while developing their key behavioural competencies and technical skills, as well as knowledge to reach their goals. But to succeed in achieving a viable career, individuals must take ownership of their work life and the choices they make along the way. Support is always beneficial, but not always readily available and reliable.

The following four helpful steps can lead a motivated individual down the right road to engaged and energised career growth.

Step 1. Developing a Career Strategy.

Without a framework or plan of approach to career development, an individual would not get very far. Too many distractions and unexpected challenges can block any movement forward. Career strategy is essential, based on employees' own awareness of what they can do, what they cannot do, and where they want to go. Knowing one's limitations, potential, and opportunities can become clearer through open and honest discussions with peers, supervisors, or mentors. Without a true assessment of the individual's personal skills and knowledge, there can be no understanding of what the employee should do (proactive steps to take) to develop the talent that the company (and the individual's goals) require. Career strategy is the foundation for individual, as well as any career development programme, success.

And above all, one needs to truly understand that luck will take a person just so far. A solid career strategy will take that individual much farther. After all, luck favours the person who is prepared.

Step 2. Possessing a Multi-Varied Skill Set and Experience.

Balancing specialisation versus gaining broader experience is no easy choice and can be very challenging for many individuals. However, if it remains unbalanced, it can also lead to stagnation over time. While altering one's function or specialising in one aspect of a field is important, today's fast-moving talent competition is more amenable to individuals who can offer an employer broad knowledge and experience with top-notch specialisation.

Finding a match in a diverse company that spans a number of industries, geographic regions, and position offerings is one way to maneuver through different opportunities to enhance one's skill level. Whatever steps are taken, make sure that they lead to the ultimate goal of having a broad array of experiences with a very solid set of specialisations. The future talent market will increasingly favour, not the most-talented in one single area but the most-talented in multiple domains.

Step 3. Discovering the Sustainable Energy Source.

Finding one's true niche is a difficult and long process but talent that provides sustainable energy and motivation is key to building a career that will last. Without an adequate energy source, nothing moves forward. But the source of that energy should be sustainable—a source that does not fade over time, a source that actually recycles itself when fed with the right elements, and a source that is deep enough and wide enough so it does not perish quickly just when the person starts.

There is nothing more important than finding that energy source and ensuring that there is enough to begin. And remember, we all have to get used to changing careers, but the energy source remains true to the individual.

Step 4. Obtaining Exposure to, and Support of, Leadership.

Having leadership support is essential to moving up the ladder or into attractive lateral positions. Just don't believe in fairy tales that say, "if you do what you like and work hard, you will get where you want to go." Although, with luck, that may happen, reality is such that without leadership support and exposure, a person will not go very far.

Therefore, it is critical that you select and only work for organisations in which leadership support or exposure is not a "special promotional event" but part of very normal daily business. Companies that are run by leaders who are able to provide real career opportunities rather than very vague and unfocused career development programmes are the only working environments you should participate in for successful career progression.

What It All Means

Sitting idly back and expecting that the employer will see one's potential and offer the right steps forward is foolhardy. Many employers try to do their best to support career development, but fall short in nudging people into the right direction. They say employees—rather than the employer—should be in charge of their own careers, totally ignoring the implications of such an approach. Very few companies are likely to partner with employees on that last mile of nudging.

The benefits of becoming truly engaged in employees' career development can be very fruitful, not only for employees but also for employers who seek continuous efficiencies in their organisations. Employers who complain about employees' engagement should also assess the level of their engagement in their employees' career progression.

The bottom line is simple: If we want to truly increase efficiency in our organisations, we should also focus on increasing the level of employers' engagement with the workforce.

CHAPTER 15

5 Lessons from Cooking to Boost Your Career

The majority of clients we work with complain about their employees' frustration in choosing a perfect career path and, therefore, remain demotivated and discouraged. We assure them the opportunities are endless, but they need to first convey the message to their employees that they should not just wait for the perfect match of job skills and position.

To determine which career path to choose is no easy task; it takes enormous self-reflection, validation, strategic oversight, and disciplined actions. Even having taken all those steps, there is no guarantee that one can always advance as planned. After all, if your plans resulted in expected outcomes, the world would be a very boring place. Surprise, unexpected outcome, success, and failure are all part of everyone's life. However, your chances of being successful and developing your career are much higher when you have a plan and a validated strategy.

Progression in one's career is a journey, not a destination. People who think of their careers as destinations—and there are quite a lot of them—end up with greater frustration down the road. This result is actually worse than if they had felt that way earlier in their careers. Those individuals who lose their motivation and energy for action and hunger for learning in any age group (without exception) because they think they have arrived at their destinations are destined to fade away.

In a world where average life expectancy[1] is constantly increasing thanks to astonishing progress in technology and social awareness, we all need to think in a radically different way about career life span and progression. At times, it becomes even ridiculous to think about traditional retirement plans. People who plan and wish to depend on these traditional plans should sincerely consider their perspectives about career progression in the long run.

Lessons from Cooking School

When you think about it, career progression is very similar to cooking. The more you practice and explore new ingredients, the better you will be in preparing the best dishes for your own taste and others. A good chef constantly seeks new combinations of good taste. Without exploring and trying new options, a good chef would not have the ability to innovate and bring new tastes to customers and remain at the top of the culinary game.

As in all fields of expertise, some chefs fail, while others become very successful. Not all chefs excel, either because they fail to carefully consider all the elements of becoming a good chef or they lose the commitment to become one. If you want to progress in

---

[1] https://en.wikipedia.org/wiki/List_of_countries_by_life_expectancy

your career—become a good chef of your career—consider the following critical lessons.

Lesson 1. Develop Technical and Soft Skills.

Without acquiring technical and soft skills needed for your dream career, you cannot master your craft. Career progression (as in cooking) does not happen by chance. You must have the technical knowledge to balance the right assortment of expertise-related ingredients and be able to determine what amount of ingredient works with another. If you use one ingredient too heavily, you can easily jeopardise the end result and serve a very unbalanced dish.

For example, you may wish to eventually become head of Information Technology (IT). Of course, you then keep up-to-date on all the latest software, hardware, research, and so on. But then you forget the importance of learning to be a good manager. So, you attend a basic course on supervising and, perhaps, budgeting, before turning your attention back to what really interests you: IT. The end result is that you may become a technological super star, but your lack of managerial skills will prove detrimental down the road.

Lesson 2. Constantly Explore New Opportunities.

Being purposefully open to opportunities is not the same thing as just bumping into them by chance. One must be open to becoming involved in new projects or initiatives, which will boost the chance of meeting new people, learning from them, and exchanging ideas. As you move outward, new opportunities are more likely to present themselves. You must be always alert to the possibilities of new skill ingredients and techniques. Without the infusion of new ideas and opportunities to broaden your expertise, your career will stagnate.

Going back to the IT career, anyone who wishes to excel in the field must always stay abreast of new developments, new programmes, and new research. If you fall behind in your knowledge and skill, your career in IT will be as short-lived as your laptop, which so quickly becomes obsolete.

Lesson 3. Cultivate End-to-End Thinking.

You simply cannot progress in your career if you view things through a single lens. Therefore, you need to develop an end-to-end view of your career. Consider a good chef, who is not only good in the kitchen but also cares about how the restaurant looks, what plates to use, how to position the restaurant in relation to the competition, and so on.

In other words, such an expansive way of thinking about your career, say, in IT, implies you need to market yourself. Developing an optimal career requires an IT expert to understand how the job fits into the overall organisation, what specific skills to offer to what particular department or company, how to position your entirety of knowledge and skills versus that of your competitors, and so on.

Lesson 4. Possess Customer Focus.

Somehow, many people forget that it is actually customers who pay their salaries regardless of the function in which they operate in the organisation. Good chefs care only about customers and how they can please them so that they come back over and over again to taste their cuisine.

As an IT expert, for example, you may forget or dismiss the effect your job performance may have on the organisation's customers or clients. If, say, you are developing a software programme that will more efficiently distribute the company products to the market, perhaps you need to be aware of the geographic regions that best suit your customer base and learn about those customers' needs.

Lesson 5. Be Visible to the Right People Who Support You.

No matter how good you are at what you do and no matter how hard you work for it, without the right exposure, you will be unable to advance in your career in this "super noisy" environment. We all experience an overload of noise, with everyone screaming to get attention and everybody talking at the same time, even when the words are meaningless. In such a noisy atmosphere, it is very difficult for people who have something serious and purposeful to be heard. Chefs face the same problem of getting exposure—and standing out from the crowd—when there is a restaurant on every corner.

Having leadership support, for example, is essential to moving up the ladder or into attractive lateral positions. Just don't believe in fairy tales that say, "if you do what you like and work hard, you will get where you want to go." Although, with luck, that may happen, reality is such that without leadership support and exposure, a person will not go very far. So, it is critical that you select and only work for organisations in which leadership support or exposure is not a "special promotional event" but part of very normal daily business. Companies that offer true career opportunities rather than ineffective career development programmes are essential for your successful advancement toward your goals.

So, as an IT professional, make sure that your managers recognise not only your expertise, but also your commitment to ongoing self-development and learning experiences to expand your knowledge base through participation in diverse IT projects and initiatives. Make a name for yourself, in a positive way, so that leadership is aware of what you can—and will—contribute to results.

The Bottom Line

The ingredients for a successful career are simple: technical skills, openness to new ideas, seeing the "big picture," customer-centricity, and exposure to leadership. These ingredients, when blended together with expert care and know-how, will boost your chances to succeed on whatever career path you decide to follow.

CHAPTER 16

Why Strategy Works to Address Misperceptions of Career Growth

Based on hundreds of appraisals and interviews with individuals of diverse gender, age, or education—while assessing their personal development (mostly career-related, but also dealing with life and self-fulfilment)—I have observed the most common problem to arise dealt with strategy (or, lack of it). In other words, many people fail to construct strategies to achieve a more fulfilling future. In fact, many people lack guidelines or frameworks that would enable them to develop effective strategies for their careers, lives, or relationships.

This observation is not as surprising as one might think, since a significant majority of people, in general, never receive formal guidelines as to how to live their lives satisfactorily or progress in their careers. Consider parenthood. Despite having numerous resources to draw upon when having a child, no parent goes to an institutional "school for parenthood," although this topic could potentially be a university degree!

The same lack of formal preparedness too often occurs with regard to decisions about what one should do in life or how to move up the job hierarchy. Typical (and practical) human behaviour leads an individual to find a job after graduation. After that, you are expected to navigate on your own to determine how to move forward, usually without a framework to help navigate the stormy weathers of your career. On the way, if you are "lucky," some people will offer their own success stories, which will prompt you to try and live those stories yourself. But that is where the flaw lies, along with the misperceptions such stories engender.

The Better Choice to Avoid Misperceptions

While success stories are encouraging, one must remember what they truly are, just stories, and not effective strategies. These positive tales are more about heroism and how one dealt with a specific situation, overcame a difficulty, and so on. Strategies, on the other hand, involve a framework, which will serve as a practical tool and guideline for dealing with any situation.

Consider this old concept: If you want to help poor people, don't give them money. Instead, teach them how to fish, thereby providing a more sustainable solution to poverty. In this analogy, "a story" would be the money, and the "framework" would be "teaching how to fish." Some people relate to an eager audience how they followed their passion, which explains their success. Or, perhaps, they became experts on a subject by studying and working 10,000 hours on it! These are all anecdotes, not frameworks, and, to be successful, everyone needs some type of framework.

Too often, as a result of these narratives, people face a number of misperceptions that are driven by "observed realities." It is critical for anyone who is currently planning to progress in their career or their personal life to consider these misperceptions and know how to effectively manage them. If unacknowledged, these misperceptions are so powerful that they interfere with our beliefs and paralyse our process of (logical reasoning) thinking. In the end, they may lead us to either over- or under-estimate what we are able to achieve.

Out of the several hundred interviews I have completed over the years, the following key—and dangerous—misperceptions emerged.

Misperception 1: People Win Lotteries, So You Think You Can, Too!

This misperception is probably the most attractive one. The idea behind it is that we observe others hitting a "lucky" strike without any explainable reason. For example, your neighbour wins a lottery, a peer gets an undeserved promotion, or friends land amazing jobs that even surprise them. If such events happen to others around us, why shouldn't they happen to us? This legitimate question—Why others and not me?—is one that everyone asks. Widely internalising this thought, many people wait for their turn one day. After all, if others were lucky, why shouldn't I be one day?

Individuals need a strategy to avoid falling prey to this false idea. While luck may certainly come your way one day, there is no guarantee. To depend on such good fortune is ultimately damaging to your ability to develop your strengths and knowledge.

My advice: Don't wait for your turn, as it will most likely never be your turn.

Misperception 2: You See Good Things Happening to Others, but Not to You.

This misperception is the most "real." Others need not win lotteries around you, but it appears that lots of other good things happen to them. In your restricted viewpoint:

- Others get promoted and earn more than you, although you think you deserve it, too.

- Others have more opportunities from which to choose, thereby boosting their career progression.

- Others have more support for reasons that are not very clear to you or anyone else.

- Others perform poorly, yet still manage to move forward at whatever they attempt.

And to make matters worse, you don't seem to be alone in this observation. Other people around you also "see" the same things, making this misperception even more powerful. Without a strategy to avoid this negative mindset, you can easily become resentful and bitter, thereby adversely affecting your own life and that of those around you.

My advice: Don't try to reason out obvious manipulation and self-interest. You will most likely never achieve favour by anyone in that type of environment. If things are not transparent in terms of who get valued or promoted, there is something fundamentally wrong in that organisation.

Misperception 3: People Get Away with Lying.

You perceive that some people escape the consequences of lying, even though you are told to practise the opposite: Tell and live the truth. The most important thing to recognise about lying is to understand why people do so in the first place. The simple answer is that people think they can get away with it! And do they? The "truthful" answer to that question is "absolutely," which is the main reason that people deceive others.

Lying is an amazing practical tool that is used as a shortcut to resolve any size problem. Its lifetime can be either very short (seconds) or as long as the truth is not discovered—which can, hypothetically, be eternity.

If you don't acknowledge this truth, the result can potentially be frustration. You can become upset with the world both within and around you, which may prove to be very destructive—for the most part, in fact, destructive to you. So, people need to acknowledge this reality and build strategies for dealing with such situations.

The main reason as to why people get stuck, frustrated, depressed, and resentful is that they are incapable of building strategies to deal with such situations. How can your boss or colleague clearly lie and get away with having whatever they want, while you choose to act with integrity and expect the same positive result, and fail to get it? It is almost an impossible expectation. However, that does not mean you should also lie to others to achieve what you desire. That choice is one you must make and pay for, either internally (by hiding yourself from the truth, while living in agony and soulless misery until you perish) or by being shamed and exposed externally in front of others one day.

My advice: Don't stay in corrupt and harmful environments. The quicker you extricate yourself from such toxic situations, the less damage you will do to yourself by not mortgaging your unrealised future potential.

Misperception 4: You Perceive Failure as Pain.

In your life or career, you attempt many things, but they don't work. Consequently, failure starts to feel like pain, which is a dangerous misperception. So many individuals refuse to be daring and try new approaches because they are afraid of failure (AKA, pain). Nobody wants to experience pain at any point, no matter the intensity.

Developing a strategy to understand failure and appreciate the lessons it may teach you is critical to going beyond that failure and achieving success. This approach is beneficial, whether dealing with personal or career decisions.

My advice: If you are seeking genuine change, you must embrace failure, which will enable you to fine-tune your framework as you develop yourself or your career. Nobody has the miracle solution to success, fulfilment, or whatever you need to live a meaningful life. No single approach offers a silver bullet.

Change Misperception to Clarity

In light of these false observations and misunderstandings that challenge us on a daily basis, one needs to be able to think clearly and comprehend the risks in what we face. When you listen to others' stories of their lucky breaks, remember, they are just telling you a nice story, but not providing a practical framework that will set you on the path you need.

Everyone needs more substance than stories in life to develop oneself on a personal basis, as well as in a satisfying work life. Everyone needs a framework—a "how to"—in order to strategise.

CHAPTER 17

5 Career Mistakes Every Employee Should Avoid

No matter the experience level and knowledge, at some point in their work life, most individuals make one or more mistakes that have the potential to derail or stall their career path. Understanding the fallacy inherent in these mistakes, or beliefs, is crucial to positioning oneself to be offered and to accept growth opportunities that can satisfy the goals and desires of both the organisation and the individual.

Mistake 1. Even Though the Definition of "Success" Is Not Clearly Defined or Communicated in Your Organisation, You Still Expect to Be Fairly Promoted.

Success means different things to different people. Consequently, it is extremely important to view the definition under a reality microscope. For example, some businesses define success as 3% to 5% growth per year, while others cite 10% to 15% or even 20%+. Accelerated career opportunities happen mostly in fast-growing business environments. That said, since the growth rate is a key indicator of career progression in any organisation, there is no point in expecting fast movement if your business is in a slow-growth industry.

Exacerbating the situation, some businesses do not provide transparency on what success means in terms of leadership career progression, as well as the company's financial viability. Without clear communication of the goals to which one should aspire, the chance to discover and take advantage of growth opportunities becomes exceedingly difficult.

Mistake 2. You Are Not Close to the Centre of the "Success" Party, But You Still Think You Are a Key Participant.

Watch carefully who are the hosts at the centre of the success party in your organisation, and observe your distance from the centre of the party. If you are at the periphery, you are simply a guest.

Rather than waiting for an invitation to each party, take responsibility in determining how to transform your role from guest to host. Discover the rules of the game, make the right connections within successful networks, take the steps to move from the periphery and ever closer toward the centre, and organise your own parties.

And in any situation, guests come and go, while hosts remain the same. If you cannot be a host in your organisation, and desire real growth opportunities, then you need to find another home.

Mistake 3. Although the Same Players Are Passed the Ball All the Time, You Are Still Waiting for Someone Who Might Pass the Ball to You.

Picture this scenario: You think that you are as talented as others in the organisation. In fact, you attend the same training sessions, participate in the same meetings, contribute the same way and as much as others do, and present yourself as part of the same team. But when it comes to new career opportunities and initiatives, no one is talking to you. In fact, no one even mentions your name.

Most of the time, management passes the "opportunity ball" to the same players in the team. Nobody gives you the opportunity to grow a business or drive a strategic project that is critical to the success of your organisation. You never get to touch the "opportunity ball" or even approach it. In fact, you are simply a spectator. Actual players and spectators enjoy the game in very different ways. Don't ever make the mistake in assuming that because you are part of a team, you will eventually get to play.

Mistake 4. Others Silently Stop Supporting You, But You Still Believe That Receiving No Feedback Is a Good Thing.

The most important point to recognise in your career is the precise moment when others "silently" stop supporting you. Failing to acknowledge this point, because of any reason—such as having a stable position, a slow but consistent salary progression, or a happy office environment—will trick your mind falsely and hamper your career.

You need to be serious, conscious, and realistic at all times on how others communicate with you and provide feedback, particularly if there is no feedback. If others silently stop supporting you, understand that it means they will not stand up for you when you need help. In truth, they may abandon you to your own devices when you are in most need of support or assistance, thereby resulting in you getting stuck in avoidable situations. After all, successful individuals go nowhere without the support of other people.

Mistake 5. You Are Not Developing Your Career Like an Entrepreneur, Yet You Still Believe That Someone Will Develop It for You.

You are not learning or doing anything to continuously improve your knowledge, expertise, and exposure to networks outside your organisation. In addition, you naively believe that just being employed actually increases your level of employability.

Don't accept mediocrity. Whatever you decide to learn, go deep so that you are able to bring fresh insights to others and receive recognition not only within your organisation, but, most importantly, outside of it. After all, you may decide to leave the company, or perhaps your employer decides to let you go. In either case, remember that your personal brand needs to be much better than your employer's brand. Although conventional wisdom dictates the opposite—that is, if you work for a good brand, it should be easier to find another position—it is absolutely not true in today's context. As jobs become more and more scarce, the importance of impactful individual contribution increases exponentially.

Others outside your organisation need to first recognise your brand, then your employer's brand. In fact, you are part of your current employer's brand. That said, if you are currently working for a good organisation, management already acknowledges that truth because they could not build a good brand without treating you as an essential component of their brand.

Take Responsibility for Your Mistakes

The bottom line is simply as follows: It is inevitable that individuals will make one or more mistakes in advancing up their career ladder. But these errors in judgment are avoidable, or, at least, repairable, if one understands why such thinking doesn't work. Individuals must take responsibility for understanding what success means to their career growth and then go after it. To achieve desired goals, employees should consider themselves as entrepreneurs, even within the confines of an employer's organisation.

Never, ever stop learning to renew yourself to become a key player. The future is so bright for those who deeply understand how important it is to believe a simple truth: It is never too late to discover new opportunities, and the only person who should care about you is you.

CHAPTER 18

The New Currency for Your Future Career Success: Relevancy

Speaking with our clients, we often emphasise the importance of staying relevant. We strongly believe that "relevancy" will become one of the most often-used words in management areas, including HR, marketing, sales, finance, operations, and others.

Consider this concept: The biggest challenge we all face in business and our professional careers involves change and its speed. Today's acceleration of speed is at a mind-boggling level. It is becoming very difficult to notice not only the velocity of change, but also the impact of the transformations happening every day. Consequently, many organisations struggle to remain relevant in their business sectors, as do many people in their jobs.

Wherein Lies the Problem?

The source of that shortcoming is what we call, "learning capability deficit." In 2017, we published *The Coming Age of Accelerated Learning*. Our purpose was to explain the reality that if people and organisations did not accelerate their learning capability, they were doomed to stay irrelevant and lag behind future competition. Our proposed framework and model for accelerated learning ensured readers that accelerated learning is only achievable through learning about one's self. Any other attempt would result in wasted resources and unnecessary pain, with tremendous hidden costs to the individual, the community, society, and employers.

Fast forward to 2020, only a three-year leap. It is astonishing to see how the importance of "relevance" is even more accentuated. The idea of remaining relevant, anchored, and driven only by one's past successes will accelerate to lose its significance in 2020 and beyond.

Think about that observation. There are already many widely accepted warnings to not depend on past successes, because they do not necessarily predict future accomplishments. Yet, this awareness is missing for many people and organisations—not because successful companies or individuals forget what made them successful and they are unable to repeat the experience. Rather, future success is increasingly becoming dependent on learning new things, faster and in an environment that changes at lightning speed. If this premise holds true, it is safe to think that we should not expect the same outcomes in the future.

In other words, if we stop learning or do not accelerate our learning capability, success is unlikely to occur as it had in the past. The reason is that we will not know how to become successful if we do not learn how to do so in a fast-changing future. As they say, "you don't know what you don't know, especially if you stop learning." And, consequently, if you stop learning, or choose to remain static, you lose relevancy.

A Simple Framework for Change and How to Remain Relevant

The future, however, is not bleak for anyone who is willing to learn. Whether as an individual or organisation, one can be progressive by making an effort to remain more relevant through this simple framework for change:

- Move your focus to what you want more of, and do more of it.
- Identify and eliminate the main source for what you no longer want.
- Establish and secure the sustainability of the future environment that you want.

Within this framework, you can take practical steps to ensure that you become, and remain, relevant:

1) Make Learning Your Biggest Investment. Ensure that education, whether through formal study or hands-on experience, is the most significant portion of your personal and organisational investment budget. Typically the most neglected area for the majority of people and organisations today, learning is an invaluable asset that will determine how relevant you are within your own domain(s).

2) Focus on the Source of Your Problems, Not the Symptoms. Only hire and work with people who are hungry to learn. Forget about the rest. The experiences, skills and knowledge acquired in the past should only serve

to assess how much the individual you are hiring or working with is eager to learn new things—not how much that person already knows or is good at performing a specific task. If you don't modify the input, don't expect to change the output.

3) Eliminate Waste to Build a More Sustainable Environment for Growth. Eliminate and avoid the leaders, managers, and employees who have no interest in learning and cultivating others. If one does not want to learn, one cannot help others to do so. The simple reality is that you cannot build an intelligent and sustainable organisation with ignorant people. To ensure real change, be ready to alter anything that is under your control. The rest is just about making excuses.

4) Empower and Guide Others Without Telling Them What to Do. Rather than telling employees or colleagues what to learn, ask them to tell you what they think they should learn. If employees are incapable of knowing what they should learn, the organisation has a much larger problem. That is the time to request help to evaluate the situation rather than wasting time and going around in circles. Don't be pretentious and tell others what they should learn without making sure that they actually think about what they should learn. Everyone needs to take ownership of their own improvement.

The Bottom Line: Relevancy

The key message is simple: Employers and clients will consider you to be simply irrelevant, if you stop learning new things and do not accelerate your learning capability. Irrelevant people or organisations think they know everything by "only" repurposing what they already know and refusing to learn new things.

Individuals and organisations that demonstrate an urgency and enthusiasm to continue their education and self-development, without depending on past successes, will increasingly own the future. It is time to participate in this new future. Don't wait until it is too late.

FINAL THOUGHTS

CHAPTER 19

5 Visions for the Future Organisation

The organisation of the future is here—or nearly so. Before it arrives, leadership and employees together should prepare. The need to secure the long-term viability of the organisation, as well as employees' own career paths and personal development, can only serve to move the organisation forward on a successful road.

Vision 1. There Will Be No "Us" vs. "Them."

Whether profit or non-profit, corporation or association, the future organisation cannot survive with an "us" vs. "them (the outside world)" mentality. If you truly understand the transformation taking place in many industries, it is evident that such thinking is absurd. The leaders who insist on keeping their organisations "cosy" for their employees, as well as themselves, will eventually become extinct for two reasons:

- Cosy cultures do not breed innovation—they are laggards—simply because they often aim at resolving problems only within the organisation and against open collaboration with the outside world. They hinder and discourage fresh ideas from new blood.

- The "we are unique and special" culture approach is totally protectionist and contrary to the diverse and agile organisation design requirements of the future.

This protectionist view and management culture is archaic, yet still followed by many organisations. Limiting growth and innovation within the boundaries of the organisation is detrimental. A key reminder that leaders often overlook is that the main purpose of the corporation is to generate value for all stakeholders—not equal, but relative, value based on potential risk and effort expended. That value can only increase through fresh and evolving concepts by being open to, and integrated with, the outside world.

Vision 2. There Will Be No Place for "Internal" Leaders.

If a person cannot lead outside of the organisation, that individual is simply a pretentious leader. The ability to lead is a characteristic that the person should be able to illustrate beyond the job—in the community, within the family, and in whatever circle with whom the leader interacts. Remarkable and successful leaders, who are recognised as leaders in their industry or area of expertise, possess these traits:

- The ability to drive major transformational change and innovative initiatives and lead others—not with their assumed authority, but due to their convincing vision and highly compelling ideas and insights.

- No fear of failure, accompanied by willingness to take highly complex, yet calculated, risks.

- The capacity to listen and the expertise to know to whom they should listen.

- The ability to move fast, with accurate information, and a focus on the best outcome for all parties.

Leaders need to be leaders wherever their expertise is required. With their ability to "shine" within their organisations, as well as in the public domain, leaders can successfully drive their organisations' efforts to achieve strategic goals.

Vision 3. Transparency in Management Will Prevail Through Technology.

Technological advancement has indirectly driven the movement toward transparency in management. As technology pushes the boundaries of maximising business profitability, it has also transformed the rules of collaboration, competitive advantage through the democratisation of creativity, and the dynamics of sharing outcomes.

The more that management practices and policies become transparent, the better and more effectively they will serve their shareholders, customers, workforce, and even communities. Yet, despite this motivation, all stakeholders do not empower, or believe in, this movement. Non-transparency triggers huge hidden costs from wasted resources, finances, and time for all parties—expenditures that many leadership teams might not be able to evaluate or recognise but that also limit the individual and organisational potential to outperform.

But whether leaders or organisations resist the movement, technology continues to accelerate the transformation to transparency in unprecedented ways. Change is inevitable and will eventually overcome resistance. The best action for employees and their leadership teams to take is to get on board now and prepare the organisation for that evolution.

Vision 4. A Multi-Talented Workforce Will Be the Norm.

A balance between soft and technical skills at every level is critical to maintain the organisation's future growth. Employees need to be good at almost everything. Although that does not mean that every individual should excel at every function, having a good working knowledge of many jobs can enable the individual to step in wherever needed and contribute to the unit's efforts. The ability to "wear different hats" will make any employee a valuable asset whom the company wishes to motivate, engage, and retain.

One way to acquire knowledge of different functions is to first identify personal strengths and weaknesses, along with specific desires for personal and career development. Through career development programmes, employees can broaden the scope of their knowledge and skills, while satisfying their own needs for job development. Multi-talents will be much in demand.

Vision 5. Keeping Up Through Accelerated Learning Will Become a "Must."

The increasing importance of learning has created an unprecedented demand for different and higher forms of understanding, awareness, and leadership. The intersection of new technologies and exponential growth of knowledge accumulation will accelerate this demand during the 21th century and beyond.

The life span of knowledge and human skills today is shorter than ever, increasing the pressure on individuals to remain at the forefront of any domain throughout one's career or a lifetime. Although some people may view "life-long learning" as merely a slogan or buzz word, it is quickly becoming a crucial factor in our evolution as individuals, educators, and employers. It is imperative to keep an open mind and continually broaden one's horizons.

The Bottom Line

What these points mean, in essence, is that leadership and the workforce should be cooperating to reach common goals—now! The future is here, or nearly so. The better prepared everyone is—through inclusion, true leadership, transparency, multiple talents, and the desire to learn—the higher the potential for long-term optimal results for both the individual and the organisation to which they belong.

CHAPTER 20

Why Generating Value for All Stakeholders Makes Business Sense

The most productive, successful organisations ensure that all stakeholders (management, employees, shareholders, and customers/clients) gain some form of value for their participation in the enterprise. Without a positive return—be it in job security, profits and revenues, productivity—the parties would turn their time, talents, and attention elsewhere.

What Each Stakeholder Wants

Each stakeholder in an enterprise has desires and needs that must be met for the organisation to move forward, to thrive, and to survive in the global marketplace. If the company is fortunate, those desires and needs overlap to an extent that encourages cooperation and shared effort toward achieving results. Consider:

- The leadership team wants the company to produce market results that earn a strong place among its competitors and peers. To reach this point, management expects employees to be innovative, highly productive, and efficient. By providing excellent products and/or services in the market, the company gains a positive public image, which, together, bring management their desired financial rewards, perquisites, and status.

- In return for their efforts and labour, employees want competitive compensation and benefits, work-life balance, feedback and communication, and an understanding of where they fit in the workings of the operation. Employees also want to know that their effort makes a difference, so that they can leave the job satisfied at the end of their work day. Security, both present and future, is also desirable to a reasonable extent.

- Shareholders spend money on corporate stock and expect a profitable return on that investment. They also want leadership teams who act with integrity, avoiding legal problems that could damage the company's standing in the community and adversely affect their investment returns. Shareholders also want communication from leadership on the state of the organisation's financial standing and future plans.

- Customers/clients want dependable, high-quality goods and services. They also require excellent customer service, with intelligent, knowledgeable, and trained employees having the authority to effectively address any problems or difficulties.

What Happens If They Do Not Get What They Want

If the different categories of stakeholders do not receive the value they legitimately expect, the consequences for the company's long-term viability may be grim. Typical scenarios, when the company fails to produce desired results, might include the following:

- Leadership may decide to cut back on resources, lay off nonessential employees, reduce or eliminate bonuses, freeze salaries, eliminate training programmes, curtail business travel, reduce research efforts, and take other actions that can eventually doom the company to stagnation.

- Employees are likely to lose their jobs; morale will drop; and employees will become disengaged and, potentially, careless, leading to poor product quality and lower profits.

- Shareholders will see stock value decline and capital gains drop, prompting them to sell their stock and invest elsewhere. In addition, they may express uncertainty and dissatisfaction about the company, thereby damaging the company's already spotty public image.

- Customers/clients, unhappy with poor quality and customer service, will take their business to the competition, reducing the enterprise's market share and revenues.

Some, all, or even more negative results can potentially occur, depending on a number of factors. If leadership is strong and willing to make an effort to engage employees in their shared dilemma, together, they may correct the company's downward spiral.

The Road to Value: Aligned Employees

That joint effort is the key to ensuring that all parties gain some form of value for their participation and investment in the company. Leadership must possess focused goals and a clear strategy first, before making the extra effort to get employees on their side. After all, having a straightforward goal, a generous budget, and skilled leadership may still not guarantee success without the support of the underlying force that drives the organisation: its workforce.

Employees, at least the majority of them, must align with leadership's desires, while ascertaining that their own needs are met. If the employee base is disengaged, if they feel unrecognised and neglected, and if they feel undervalued, they will not truly care what management wants. In fact, they may not even know what their work efforts are striving towards.

The road to that joint effort of successful cooperation begins with knowledge and information, regarding whether employees are a "fit" with the company's culture, as well as with their present occupation. Without that awareness, employees will come to work, perform a less-than-stellar job, and produce inferior results. But, possessing that knowledge, they will enter the office or factory or field site with motivation, energy, and the power to ensure that the company will generate value for all stakeholders.

REFERENCES

Wikipedia.org   Chapter 12

The Coming Age of Accelerated Learning   Chapter 18

INDEX

Topic	Chapter
Challenges	Chapter 9
Clarity	Chapter 3, 13
Competitiveness	Chapter 11
Cost	Chapter 3
Growth	Chapter 12
HR manager	Chapter 3, 8
Leadership	Chapter 13
Mindset	Introduction
Misalignment	Chapter 9
Mistakes	Chapter 17
Networks	Chapter 11, 12
Relevancy	Chapter 18
Right people	Chapter 2, 3
Rules	Chapter 10
Self-Knowledge	Chapter 6, 8, 9, 13
Strategy	Chapter 5, 8, 12, 14, 16
Talent	Chapter 2, 3, 4, 5
Transparency	Chapter 13

Value generation	Chapter 20
Visions	Chapter 19

www.ingramcontent.com/pod-product-compliance
Lightning Source LLC
Chambersburg PA
CBHW021434210526
45463CB00002B/507